How to Make Traditional Dishes:

Central America

David J Garcia

Table of Contents

Introduction

Welcome to a culinary journey through the heart of Central America! This cookbook is a celebration of the vibrant and diverse tapestry of flavors that define the rich gastronomic heritage of this region. From the lush rainforests to the serene coasts, Central America's cuisine reflects its history, culture, and natural bounty. Through this collection of traditional recipes, we invite you to explore and savor the essence of Central American cooking, rooted in centuries of tradition and cherished family recipes passed down through generations.

A Tapestry of Flavors

Central American cuisine is a fusion of indigenous traditions, European influences, and African and Asian flavors brought by migration and trade. It's a culinary mosaic that varies from country to country, yet shares a unifying thread of fresh ingredients, bold spices, and techniques that have stood the test of time. From the fiery chilies of Mexico to the savory stews of Guatemala, each dish is a reflection of the region's cultural diversity and history.

The Heart of Every Home

In Central America, food is more than sustenance; it is a cornerstone of social gatherings and familial bonds. Cooking is an act of love, and every dish tells a story—a tale of heritage, resilience, and community. Whether it's the aromas of spices filling the air during festivals or the warmth of a family kitchen, the preparation and sharing of food form an integral part of everyday life.

Exploring Central American Cuisine

This cookbook is a gateway to exploring the flavors and aromas of Central America. You'll discover recipes that span from the mountains of Honduras to the coastal regions of Belize, each offering a glimpse into the unique culinary traditions of the area. From tantalizing street foods to comforting home-cooked meals, these recipes have been carefully selected to showcase the diversity and authenticity of Central American cuisine.

Embracing Authenticity

Authenticity is at the heart of this cookbook. While we've curated these recipes to be accessible to home cooks, we've also strived to maintain the integrity and essence of each dish. Throughout these pages, you'll find tips on sourcing traditional ingredients and mastering cooking techniques that are central to achieving the authentic flavors of Central America.

A Culinary Adventure

Embark on a culinary adventure as we guide you through the preparation of classic Central American dishes. Whether you're a seasoned chef or a novice in the kitchen, these recipes are designed to inspire and delight your taste buds. Gather fresh produce, spices, and your sense of culinary curiosity as we venture into the world of Central American cooking together.

Celebrating Tradition

As we delve into this cookbook, let's honor the culinary legacies passed down through generations. Each recipe encapsulates the spirit of Central American kitchens, preserving tradition while inviting creativity. So, roll up your sleeves, embrace the aromas, and let's embark on a flavorful journey that pays homage to the vibrant tapestry of Central American cuisine.

Get ready to explore the enchanting flavors and cultural richness of Central America —one plate at a time.

Section 1

Belize

Chicken Stew

Serves: 4-6   Prep time: 15 min   Cook time: 1 hr

INGREDIENTS

3 pounds of chicken pieces (thighs, legs, or a whole chicken cut into pieces)

2 tablespoons of cooking oil

1 onion, finely chopped

2 cloves of garlic, minced

1/2 cup of bell pepper, finely chopped

1/2 cup of green onions (scallions), chopped

1/4 cup of tomato sauce or ketchup

1 teaspoon of thyme leaves (fresh or dried)

1 teaspoon of allspice (pimento) or ground cloves

1/2 teaspoon of black pepper

1/2 teaspoon of salt

1-2 habanero or scotch bonnet peppers, finely chopped (adjust to your preferred level of spiciness)

1/4 cup of vinegar

2 cups of water

Optional: 1-2 bay leaves

DIRECTIONS

1. **Marinate the Chicken:**
    - In a large bowl, combine the chicken pieces with the vinegar. Let it marinate for about 10 minutes. This helps to remove any gamey taste from the chicken.
2. **Sauté Aromatics:**
    - In a large, heavy-bottomed pot, heat the cooking oil over medium heat.
    - Add the chopped onion, garlic, bell pepper, green onions, and habanero or scotch bonnet peppers. Sauté for a few minutes until they become fragrant and slightly softened.
3. **Add Chicken:**
    - Add the marinated chicken pieces to the pot and brown them on all sides for about 5-7 minutes.
4. **Season the Chicken:**
    - Stir in the tomato sauce (or ketchup), thyme leaves, allspice (or ground cloves), black pepper, and salt. You can also add bay leaves for extra flavor.
    - Continue to cook, stirring, for a few more minutes to coat the chicken with the seasonings.
5. **Simmer:**
    - Pour in 2 cups of water and bring the mixture to a gentle boil.
    - Reduce the heat to low, cover the pot, and let it simmer for about 30-40 minutes, or until the chicken is tender and the sauce has thickened. Stir occasionally.
6. **Serve:**
    - Belizean Stew Chicken is typically served with Belizean Rice and Beans, but it can also be enjoyed with white rice or tortillas.

Enjoy this flavorful Belizean dish, rich in spices and seasonings! Adjust the level of spiciness by adding more or fewer habanero or scotch bonnet peppers to suit your taste.

Fried Plantains

Serves: 2-4 Prep time: 5 min Cook time: 15 min

INGREDIENTS

2 ripe (yellow to black) plantains

2 tablespoons of cooking oil (vegetable or canola oil)

Salt, to taste (optional)

Optional for garnish: powdered cinnamon or sugar

DIRECTIONS

1. Select and Prepare the Plantains:
   - Choose ripe plantains with yellow to black skins. Ripe plantains should be soft to the touch and have some black spots or streaks on the skin.
   - Peel the plantains by making a lengthwise slit in the skin and then peeling it away. Slice the plantains into rounds, about 1/2 inch (1.3 cm) thick. You can also slice them diagonally if you prefer a different shape.

2. **Heat the Oil:**
    - In a frying pan or skillet, heat the cooking oil over medium-high heat. The oil should be hot but not smoking.
3. **Fry the Plantains:**
    - Carefully add the sliced plantains to the hot oil. Be cautious as the oil may splatter a bit.
    - Fry the plantains for about 2-3 minutes on each side, or until they turn golden brown and crispy. Use a spatula to flip them.
4. **Drain Excess Oil:**
    - Once the plantains are fried to your desired level of crispiness, use a slotted spoon to remove them from the oil. Place them on a plate lined with paper towels to drain any excess oil.
5. **Season and Serve:**
    - If you like, sprinkle the fried plantains with a pinch of salt for a savory touch.
    - For a sweeter version, you can dust the plantains with a bit of powdered cinnamon or sugar while they are still hot.
    - Serve the Belizean Fry Ripe Plantains as a side dish, snack, or dessert.

Belizean Fry Ripe Plantains are a delightful combination of sweet and savory, and they make a delicious accompaniment to various meals or can be enjoyed on their own.

Rice and Beans

Serves: 4-6 Prep time: 15 min Cook time: 1.5 hrs

INGREDIENTS

1 cup of red kidney beans

2 cups of long-grain white rice

1 cup of coconut milk

1 small onion, finely chopped

2 cloves of garlic, minced

1/2 cup of bell pepper, finely chopped

1/2 cup of green onions (scallions), chopped

2 tablespoons of cooking oil

1 teaspoon of thyme leaves (fresh or dried)

1 teaspoon of black pepper

1 teaspoon of salt

2 cups of water (for boiling the beans)

Optional: 1-2 habanero or scotch bonnet peppers (whole, for flavor)

DIRECTIONS

1. Soak the Red Kidney Beans:

- Rinse the red kidney beans in cold water and remove any debris or small stones.
- Place the beans in a large bowl, cover them with water, and let them soak overnight or for at least 6 hours. This will help soften the beans for cooking.

2. Cook the Red Kidney Beans:

- After soaking, drain the beans and transfer them to a large pot.
- Add 2 cups of water to the pot, along with the whole habanero or scotch bonnet pepper for flavor (remove it later if you want less heat).
- Bring the beans to a boil, then reduce the heat to a simmer, cover the pot, and let them cook for about 45 minutes to 1 hour, or until they are tender but not mushy. Add more water if needed during cooking.
- Season the beans with 1/2 teaspoon of salt during the last 15 minutes of cooking.
- Once the beans are cooked, remove and discard the pepper and drain any excess water.

3. Prepare the Coconut Milk:

- In a separate container, mix the coconut milk with an equal amount of water to create a diluted coconut milk mixture.

4. Sauté Aromatics:

- In a large, heavy-bottomed pot, heat the cooking oil over medium heat.
- Add the chopped onion, garlic, bell pepper, and green onions. Sauté for a few minutes until they become fragrant and slightly softened.

5. Add Rice and Beans:

- Stir in the washed rice and cooked red kidney beans into the pot with the sautéed aromatics.
- Pour in the diluted coconut milk mixture, and add the remaining 1/2 teaspoon of salt, black pepper, and thyme leaves.
- Stir everything well to combine.

6. **Simmer and Cook:**

- Bring the mixture to a gentle boil, then reduce the heat to low.
- Cover the pot and let it simmer for about 20-25 minutes or until the rice is tender and has absorbed the coconut milk. Avoid stirring the rice too much to prevent it from becoming sticky.

7. Serve:

- Once the rice is cooked, fluff it with a fork and serve your delicious Belizean Rice and Beans as a side dish with stewed chicken, pork, or fish.

Enjoy this traditional Belizean dish with your favorite protein and some hot sauce for an extra kick!

Tamales

Serves: 14pcs Prep time: 1hr Cook time: 2.5 hrs

INGREDIENTS

For the Filling:

2 pounds of boneless chicken, pork, or a combination of both, cut into small pieces

1 medium onion, chopped

2 cloves of garlic, minced

1 bell pepper, chopped

2 tablespoons of achiote (annatto) paste or powder

1 teaspoon of thyme leaves (fresh or dried)

1 teaspoon of allspice (pimento) or ground cloves

Salt and black pepper, to taste

2 tablespoons of cooking oil

2 cups of water or chicken broth

For the Corn Dough (Masa):

4 cups of masa harina (corn masa flour)

2 cups of chicken or pork broth (from the filling)

1 cup of vegetable oil

1 teaspoon of salt

Banana leaves or corn husks (for wrapping the tamales)

Kitchen twine (for tying the tamales)

DIRECTIONS

1. **Prepare the Filling:**
    - In a large pot, heat the cooking oil over medium heat.
    - Add the chopped onion, garlic, and bell pepper. Sauté until they become fragrant and soft.
    - Add the achiote paste or powder, thyme, allspice, salt, and black pepper. Stir to combine.
    - Add the chicken or pork pieces and cook until they are browned on all sides.
    - Pour in 2 cups of water or chicken broth, bring to a boil, and then reduce the heat to low. Cover and simmer for about 1.5 to 2 hours or until the meat is tender and can be easily shredded.
    - Once cooked, shred the meat and set it aside along with the broth.
2. **Prepare the Corn Dough (Masa):**
    - In a large mixing bowl, combine the masa harina, vegetable oil, and salt.
    - Gradually add the chicken or pork broth (from the filling) while kneading the dough until it reaches a soft, pliable consistency. If needed, add more broth or water to achieve the right texture.
3. **Prepare the Banana Leaves or Corn Husks:**
    - Soften banana leaves or corn husks by soaking them in hot water for about 15-20 minutes. Then, dry them off with a towel.

4. **Assemble the Tamales:**
   - Take a softened banana leaf or corn husk and spread a small portion of the corn dough on it. Add a spoonful of the shredded meat filling on top of the dough.
   - Carefully fold the banana leaf or corn husk over the filling to create a rectangular package. Fold up the bottom, then fold in the sides, and tie the tamale with kitchen twine.
5. **Steam the Tamales:**
   - In a large steamer, arrange the tamales vertically with the folded side down.
   - Steam the tamales for about 1 hour until the dough is cooked and firm. Check occasionally and add more water to the steamer if needed.
6. **Serve:**
   - Let the tamales cool for a few minutes before unwrapping them. Serve your Belizean Tamales warm and enjoy!

Belizean Tamales are a labor of love, but the result is a delicious and flavorful dish that's perfect for special occasions and gatherings. The quantity of tamales may vary depending on the size of each tamale.

Chimole

Serves: 4-6 Prep time: 20 min Cook time: 40 min

INGREDIENTS

For the Black Sauce:

3 tablespoons of annatto seeds (achiote)

3 tablespoons of black recado paste (available at Latin grocery stores or make your own)

2 tablespoons of vegetable oil

1 medium onion, finely chopped

2 cloves of garlic, minced

1 bell pepper, finely chopped

2-3 tomatoes, chopped

1-2 habanero or scotch bonnet peppers, finely chopped (adjust to your preferred level of spiciness)

1 teaspoon of allspice (pimento) or ground cloves

1 teaspoon of thyme leaves (fresh or dried)

1 teaspoon of black pepper

1 teaspoon of salt

2 cups of water or beef/chicken broth

For Serving:

Cooked white rice

Corn tortillas

Sliced avocado

Sliced cucumber

Chopped cilantro

Lime wedges

DIRECTIONS

1. **Prepare the Black Sauce:**
   - Heat the vegetable oil in a large pot or Dutch oven over medium heat.
   - Add the annatto seeds and black recado paste to the hot oil. Stir them together until the oil takes on a rich red color from the annatto seeds and the recado paste is well mixed in.
   - Add the chopped onion, garlic, bell pepper, and tomatoes to the pot. Sauté until the vegetables become soft and fragrant.
2. **Add Spices and Peppers:**
   - Stir in the habanero or scotch bonnet peppers, allspice, thyme, black pepper, and salt.
3. **Create the Black Sauce:**
   - Gradually add the water or beef/chicken broth to the pot while stirring continuously. This mixture will create the black sauce (chimole). Continue to stir until the sauce thickens and all the ingredients are well combined.
4. **Simmer:**

Reduce the heat to low, cover the pot, and let the chimole simmer for about 20-30 minutes, allowing the flavors to meld together. If the sauce becomes too thick, you can add a little more water to reach your desired consistency.

5. Serve:

- Serve the chimole over white rice with warm corn tortillas.
- Offer sliced avocado, cucumber, chopped cilantro, and lime wedges as side accompaniments.

Belizean chimole is a delicious and hearty dish with a deep, savory flavor. The spiciness can be adjusted to your preference by controlling the amount of habanero or scotch bonnet peppers you use. Enjoy this traditional Belizean dish!

Ceviche

Serves: 4-6 Prep time: 30 min Cook time: N/A

INGREDIENTS

For the Ceviche:

1 pound of fresh seafood (conch, shrimp, or firm white fish), diced into small pieces

1 cup of freshly squeezed lime juice (about 10-12 limes)

1/2 cup of orange juice

1/2 cup of red onion, finely chopped

1/2 cup of bell pepper (any color), finely chopped

1/4 cup of fresh cilantro, chopped

2-3 habanero or scotch bonnet peppers, finely chopped (adjust to your preferred level of spiciness)

1-2 cloves of garlic, minced

Salt and black pepper, to taste

For Serving:

Tortilla chips or saltines

Sliced cucumber or avocado (optional)

DIRECTIONS

1. **Prepare the Seafood:**
   - If using conch, make sure it's cleaned and tenderized properly. For shrimp, peel and devein them. If using fish, ensure it's skinned and deboned. Dice the seafood into small pieces.
2. **Marinate the Seafood:**
   - In a non-metallic bowl, combine the diced seafood with the freshly squeezed lime juice. Make sure the seafood is completely submerged in the juice. Cover the bowl and refrigerate it for about 2-3 hours to allow the lime juice to "cook" the seafood. The seafood will turn opaque and take on a firm texture.
3. **Prepare the Ceviche Mix:**
   - Drain most of the lime juice from the marinated seafood, leaving just a bit to maintain the flavor. This is a crucial step as too much juice can overpower the ceviche.
   - Add the orange juice, finely chopped red onion, bell pepper, cilantro, habanero or scotch bonnet peppers, minced garlic, and a dash of salt and black pepper. Mix everything well to combine.
4. **Adjust Seasonings:**
   - Taste the ceviche and adjust the salt, pepper, and spiciness level if needed.
5. **Chill:**
   - Cover the ceviche and return it to the refrigerator to chill for an additional 30 minutes to an hour. This allows the flavors to meld together.
6. **Serve:**
   - Serve your Belizean Ceviche in small bowls or cups, garnished with slices of cucumber or avocado, if desired.
   - Accompany with tortilla chips or saltines for scooping and enjoy!

Belizean ceviche is a delightful and refreshing dish that showcases the fresh flavors of the sea. It's a perfect appetizer or snack for warm, tropical days. Adjust the level of spiciness to suit your taste by adding more or fewer habanero or scotch bonnet peppers.

Salbutes

Serves: 4-6 Prep time: 30 min Cook time: 30 min

INGREDIENTS

For the Dough:

2 cups of masa harina (corn masa flour)

1/2 teaspoon of salt

1/2 teaspoon of baking powder

1 1/4 cups of warm water

For Topping:

1/2 pound of cooked and shredded chicken, pork, or beef (or a combination)

1/2 cup of red onion, thinly sliced

1/4 cup of fresh cilantro, chopped

1/4 cup of crumbled queso fresco (or feta cheese as a substitute)

1-2 habanero or scotch bonnet peppers, thinly sliced (adjust to your preferred level of spiciness)

Lime wedges

Vegetable oil for frying

Salt and black pepper, to taste

For Serving:

Sliced avocado (optional)

Pickled onions (optional)

Hot sauce (optional)

DIRECTIONS

1. **Prepare the Dough:**
   - In a mixing bowl, combine the masa harina, salt, and baking powder.
   - Gradually add the warm water and knead the mixture until it forms a smooth, elastic dough. If it's too dry, add a little more water; if it's too sticky, add more masa harina.
   - Divide the dough into golf ball-sized portions and cover them with a damp cloth to prevent drying out.
2. **Form the Salbutes:**
   - Take one of the masa harina dough portions and flatten it into a small round shape (about 4-5 inches in diameter). You can use a tortilla press or a rolling pin.
   - Heat some vegetable oil in a skillet over medium-high heat.
   - Carefully place the flattened dough in the hot oil and fry it until it's puffy and golden brown, about 1-2 minutes on each side. Remove and drain on paper towels.
3. **Prepare the Toppings:**
   - Season the cooked and shredded chicken, pork, or beef with salt and black pepper to taste.
   - Slice the red onion, chop the cilantro, crumble the queso fresco, and slice the habanero or scotch bonnet peppers.
4. **Assemble the Salbutes:**
   - Top each fried masa harina disk with the seasoned meat, sliced red onion, chopped cilantro, crumbled queso fresco, and thinly sliced habanero or scotch bonnet peppers.
   - Squeeze some lime juice over the toppings for added flavor.
5. **Serve:**
   - Serve your Belizean Salbutes with optional accompaniments like sliced avocado, pickled onions, and hot sauce.

Belizean Salbutes are a delicious and colorful dish, featuring crispy masa harina discs topped with a variety of flavorful ingredients. Enjoy the combination of textures and flavors in this traditional Belizean treat!

Cochinita Pibil

Serves: 8-10 Prep time: 30 min Cook time: 4 hrs

INGREDIENTS

For the Marinade:

3-4 pounds of boneless pork shoulder or pork butt, cut into large chunks

2 tablespoons of achiote (annatto) paste

3-4 cloves of garlic, minced

2 teaspoons of ground cumin

2 teaspoons of dried oregano

1 teaspoon of ground allspice (pimento)

1/2 teaspoon of ground cloves

1/2 teaspoon of ground cinnamon

1/4 teaspoon of ground black pepper

Juice of 3-4 bitter oranges (or substitute with a mix of orange and lime juice)

1/4 cup of white vinegar

Salt, to taste

For Cooking:

Banana leaves (or aluminum foil if banana leaves are not available)

Cooking twine

Large roasting pan or Dutch oven

Water

For Serving:

Corn tortillas

Pickled red onions

Sliced avocado

Fresh cilantro leaves

Lime wedges

Hot sauce (optional)

DIRECTIONS

1. **Prepare the Marinade:**
   - In a mixing bowl, combine the achiote paste, minced garlic, ground cumin, dried oregano, ground allspice, ground cloves, ground cinnamon, ground black pepper, bitter orange juice, and white vinegar. Mix everything well.
2. **Marinate the Pork:**
   - Place the chunks of pork in a large resealable plastic bag or a non-metallic container.
   - Pour the marinade over the pork and make sure it's evenly coated. Seal the bag or container and marinate the pork in the refrigerator for at least 4 hours or overnight for the best flavor.
3. **Preheat the Oven:**
   - Preheat your oven to 325°F (163°C).
4. **Assemble and Cook the Cochinita Pibil:**
   - If you have banana leaves, briefly heat them over an open flame or in a hot oven to make them more pliable. If not, you can use aluminum foil.
   - Place the banana leaves (or aluminum foil) in the bottom of a large roasting pan or Dutch oven. This will help prevent the pork from sticking and infuse flavor.

- Remove the pork from the marinade, reserving the marinade.
- Place the marinated pork on top of the banana leaves (or aluminum foil).
- Pour the reserved marinade over the pork.
- Fold the banana leaves (or aluminum foil) over the pork, creating a secure packet.
- Tie the packet with cooking twine to keep it sealed.

5. **Cook the Cochinita Pibil:**
   - Place the sealed packet in the preheated oven.
   - Cook for 3-4 hours, or until the pork is tender and easily shreds with a fork.
6. **Serve:**
   - Serve the Belizean Cochinita Pibil by shredding the tender pork and serving it on corn tortillas.
   - Garnish with pickled red onions, sliced avocado, fresh cilantro leaves, lime wedges, and hot sauce, if desired.

Belizean Cochinita Pibil is a flavorful and aromatic dish with a rich marinade that infuses the pork with delicious, savory notes. Enjoy this traditional Belizean recipe with your favorite toppings!

Panades

Serves: 4-6 Prep time: 30 min Cook time: 30 min

INGREDIENTS

For the Dough:

2 cups of masa harina (corn masa flour)

1 teaspoon of salt

1/2 teaspoon of baking powder

1 cup of warm water

For the Filling:

1/2 pound of boneless fish (snapper, kingfish, or any white fish), finely chopped

1/2 cup of red onion, finely chopped

1/4 cup of bell pepper, finely chopped

2-3 cloves of garlic, minced

1-2 habanero or scotch bonnet peppers, finely chopped (adjust to your preferred level of spiciness)

1/4 cup of fresh cilantro, chopped

1/4 cup of lime juice

Salt and black pepper, to taste

For Serving:

Pickled onions (optional)

Hot sauce (optional)

DIRECTIONS

1. **Prepare the Dough:**
   - In a mixing bowl, combine the masa harina, salt, and baking powder.
   - Gradually add the warm water and knead the mixture until it forms a smooth, elastic dough. If it's too dry, add a little more water; if it's too sticky, add more masa harina.
   - Divide the dough into golf ball-sized portions and cover them with a damp cloth to prevent drying out.
2. **Prepare the Filling:**
   - In a separate bowl, combine the finely chopped fish, red onion, bell pepper, minced garlic, habanero or scotch bonnet peppers, cilantro, and lime juice.
   - Season the mixture with salt and black pepper to taste. Mix everything well and let it marinate for about 10-15 minutes.
3. **Form the Panades:**
   - Take one of the masa harina dough portions and flatten it into a small circle (about 4 inches in diameter) on a piece of plastic wrap or a banana leaf.
   - Place a spoonful of the fish filling in the center of the dough.
4. **Fold and Seal:**
   - Carefully fold the dough over the filling to create a half-moon shape.
   - Press the edges together to seal the panades, ensuring they don't open during cooking.
5. **Cook the Panades:**
   - In a large skillet, heat a few tablespoons of cooking oil over medium heat.
   - Fry the panades until they're golden brown and crispy on both sides, about 3-4 minutes per side.
   - Place the cooked panades on paper towels to remove any excess oil.

6. **Serve:**

- Serve the Belizean Panades with pickled onions and hot sauce, if desired.

Belizean Panades are a popular snack or appetizer, featuring a delightful combination of corn dough and flavorful fish filling. Enjoy these savory treats with a bit of spice and tang!

Garnaches

Serves: 4   Prep time: 15 min   Cook time: 15 min

INGREDIENTS

8 small corn tortillas

1 can (15 oz) refried red or black beans

1 cup shredded cheese (queso fresco or cheddar)

1 small onion, finely chopped

1 tomato, diced

1/2 cup pickled jalapeños or hot peppers (optional)

Vegetable oil for frying

Salt and pepper to taste

Chopped cilantro for garnish (optional)

DIRECTIONS

1. **Prepare the Garnaches:**
    - Heat a small amount of vegetable oil in a skillet over medium heat.
    - Lightly fry the corn tortillas, one at a time, for about 30 seconds on each side until they're slightly crispy. Set them aside on paper towels to drain excess oil.
2. **Assemble the Garnaches:**
    - Spread a spoonful of refried beans evenly onto each fried tortilla.
    - Sprinkle shredded cheese on top of the beans while they're still warm, allowing it to slightly melt.
    - Add a layer of chopped onions, diced tomatoes, and pickled jalapeños or hot peppers if using.
    - Season with salt and pepper to taste.
3. **Serve:**
    - Garnaches are typically served warm and can be topped with chopped cilantro for added freshness.
    - Serve them as a snack or appetizer. They are often enjoyed with hot sauce or other condiments on the side.

Belizean Garnaches are customizable, so feel free to add other toppings like shredded chicken, cabbage, or avocado slices according to your preferences. They're a delightful treat that captures the flavors of Belizean street food. Enjoy your homemade Garnaches!

Fry Jacks

Serves: 4-6 Prep time: 15 min Cook time: 15 min

INGREDIENTS

2 cups of all-purpose flour

1 teaspoon of baking powder

1/2 teaspoon of salt

2 tablespoons of vegetable shortening or butter

3/4 cup of water

Cooking oil for frying (vegetable oil or canola oil)

Optional: Honey or jam for serving

DIRECTIONS

1. Prepare the Dough:
   - In a mixing bowl, combine the all-purpose flour, baking powder, and salt. Mix them together.

2. **Add Shortening or Butter:**
   - Add the vegetable shortening or butter to the dry ingredients. Using your fingers or a pastry cutter, work the shortening into the flour mixture until it resembles coarse crumbs.
3. **Add Water:**
   - Gradually add the water to the mixture and knead it until a soft, elastic dough forms. You may need to adjust the amount of water slightly, so add it a little at a time.
4. **Rest the Dough:**
   - Cover the dough with a clean kitchen towel and let it rest for about 10-15 minutes. This allows the dough to relax and become more pliable.
5. **Roll Out the Dough:**
   - On a floured surface, roll out the dough to about 1/4-inch thickness.
6. **Cut and Shape the Fry Jacks:**
   - Use a knife or a round cutter to cut the dough into small rounds or squares, about 3-4 inches in diameter.
7. **Heat the Oil:**
   - In a deep skillet or frying pan, heat about 1 inch of cooking oil over medium-high heat until it reaches around 350°F (175°C).
8. **Fry the Fry Jacks:**
   - Carefully add the cut pieces of dough to the hot oil, a few at a time. Fry them for about 2-3 minutes on each side or until they puff up and turn golden brown. Use a slotted spoon to flip them over and remove them from the oil.
9. **Drain and Serve:**
   - Place the fried dough on a plate lined with paper towels to drain any excess oil.
   - Serve the Belizean Fry Jacks warm with honey or jam, if desired.

Belizean Fry Jacks are a popular breakfast item and snack in Belize. They are light, airy, and can be enjoyed with sweet or savory toppings, making them a versatile and delicious treat.

Section 2

Costa Rica

Gallo Pinto

Serves: 4 Prep time: 15 min Cook time: 15 min

INGREDIENTS

1 cup of cooked white rice (preferably day-old rice)

1 cup of cooked black beans (you can use canned beans or cook dried beans and drain them)

2 tablespoons of vegetable oil

1/2 cup of onion, finely chopped

1/2 cup of bell pepper (any color), finely chopped

2 cloves of garlic, minced

1 teaspoon of ground cumin

1/2 teaspoon of paprika

2 tablespoons of Salsa Lizano (or Worcestershire sauce as a substitute)

Salt and black pepper, to taste

Fresh cilantro leaves, chopped, for garnish (optional)

Sliced lime, for garnish (optional)

Fried or scrambled eggs, for serving (optional)

DIRECTIONS

1. **Prepare the Ingredients:**
   - If you're using canned black beans, make sure to drain and rinse them.
   - Chop the onion, bell pepper, and garlic.
   - Measure out the cooked white rice and set it aside.
2. **Sauté the Aromatics:**
   - In a large skillet or frying pan, heat the vegetable oil over medium-high heat.
   - Add the chopped onion and bell pepper and sauté for about 2-3 minutes until they become soft and translucent.
   - Add the minced garlic and continue to cook for another 1-2 minutes until fragrant.
3. **Add the Rice and Beans:**
   - Add the cooked white rice and black beans to the skillet with the sautéed aromatics.
   - Stir well to combine all the ingredients.
4. **Season the Gallo Pinto:**
   - Sprinkle the ground cumin and paprika over the mixture.
   - Pour the Salsa Lizano (or Worcestershire sauce) evenly over the rice and beans.
   - Season with salt and black pepper to taste.
   - Stir everything together to ensure even seasoning.
5. **Cook and Stir:**
   - Continue to cook and stir the mixture over medium heat for about 5-7 minutes. This allows the flavors to meld together and the gallo pinto to become hot and thoroughly mixed.
6. **Serve:**
   - Serve the Costa Rican Gallo Pinto hot, garnished with fresh cilantro leaves and slices of lime if desired.
   - It's often served as a side dish or with fried or scrambled eggs for a traditional Costa Rican breakfast called "Gallo Pinto con Huevo."

Costa Rican Gallo Pinto is a beloved and classic dish that can be enjoyed as a hearty breakfast or a flavorful side dish for lunch or dinner. It's a staple of Costa Rican cuisine and is incredibly delicious!

Chifrijo

Serves: 4-6 Prep time: 15 min Cook time: N/A

INGREDIENTS

For the Chifrijo:

1 cup of white rice, cooked and cooled

1 cup of black beans, cooked and drained

1/2 cup of chicharrones (pork cracklings), coarsely chopped

1/2 cup of pico de gallo (a salsa made from chopped tomatoes, onions, cilantro, lime juice, and chili peppers)

1/4 cup of Lizano sauce (or substitute with Worcestershire sauce)

1/4 cup of cooked and crumbled bacon

1/4 cup of avocado, diced

2 tablespoons of vegetable oil

2 cloves of garlic, minced

Salt and black pepper, to taste

Sliced lime, for garnish

Fresh cilantro leaves, for garnish

For Serving:

Tortilla chips

DIRECTIONS

1. **Prepare the Chifrijo Base:**
   - In a large mixing bowl, combine the cooked white rice and cooked black beans. Mix them together well.
2. **Prepare the Sautéed Garlic:**
   - In a small skillet, heat the vegetable oil over medium heat.
   - Add the minced garlic and sauté for about 1 minute, just until it becomes fragrant. Be careful not to brown the garlic.
3. **Mix the Chifrijo:**
   - Pour the sautéed garlic and oil over the rice and beans mixture.
   - Add the chopped chicharrones, pico de gallo, Lizano sauce (or Worcestershire sauce), crumbled bacon, and diced avocado.
   - Season the chifrijo with salt and black pepper to taste.
4. **Toss and Serve:**
   - Gently toss all the ingredients together until they are well mixed and coated with the sauces.
5. **Garnish and Serve:**
   - Garnish the Costa Rican Chifrijo with fresh cilantro leaves and slices of lime.
   - Serve with tortilla chips for scooping and enjoy!

Costa Rican Chifrijo is a delicious and hearty dish that combines the flavors and textures of rice, beans, chicharrones, and fresh toppings. It's often served as an appetizer or a popular bar snack in Costa Rica. Enjoy the mix of flavors and the crunch of the chicharrones with tortilla chips!

Rondon

Serves: 6-8 Prep time: 20 min Cook time: 50 min

INGREDIENTS

2 tablespoons of vegetable oil

1 onion, finely chopped

3 cloves of garlic, minced

1 bell pepper (any color), chopped

2 cups of coconut milk

2 cups of chicken or fish broth

1 cup of yam or sweet potato, peeled and diced

1 cup of cassava (yuca), peeled and diced

1 cup of green plantains, peeled and sliced

1 cup of ripe plantains, peeled and sliced

1 cup of carrots, peeled and sliced

1 cup of malanga, peeled and diced (optional)

1 pound of white fish (snapper, grouper, or similar), cut into chunks

1/2 pound of shrimp, peeled and deveined

1/2 pound of mussels or clams (optional)
Salt and black pepper, to taste
1-2 tablespoons of fresh cilantro, chopped
Lime wedges, for serving

DIRECTIONS

1. **Sauté the Aromatics:**
   - In a large pot or Dutch oven, heat the vegetable oil over medium-high heat.
   - Add the chopped onion, minced garlic, and bell pepper. Sauté until they become soft and fragrant, about 3-4 minutes.
2. **Add Coconut Milk and Broth:**
   - Pour in the coconut milk and chicken or fish broth. Stir well to combine.
3. **Add Root Vegetables:**
   - Add the diced yam or sweet potato, cassava, green plantains, ripe plantains, carrots, and malanga (if using). These are the starchy ingredients that give rondón its characteristic texture.
4. **Simmer:**
   - Cover the pot and simmer the mixture over medium heat for about 20-30 minutes, or until the root vegetables are tender.
5. **Add Seafood:**
   - Once the root vegetables are tender, add the chunks of white fish, shrimp, and mussels or clams (if using).
   - Continue to simmer until the seafood is cooked through, which should take about 5-7 minutes.
6. **Season and Garnish:**
   - Season the rondón with salt and black pepper to taste.
   - Garnish with fresh cilantro.

7. **Serve:**

- Serve the Costa Rican Rondón hot, accompanied by lime wedges for an extra burst of flavor.

Costa Rican Rondón is a hearty and flavorful stew that combines the rich and creamy texture of coconut milk with a variety of root vegetables and fresh seafood. It's a comforting dish, perfect for sharing with family and friends. Enjoy!

Casado

Serves: 4 Prep time: 30 min Cook time: 45 min

INGREDIENTS

For the Black Beans:

1 cup of black beans (you can use canned beans or cook dried beans and drain them)

1 small onion, chopped

2 cloves of garlic, minced

1 red bell pepper, chopped

1/2 teaspoon of ground cumin

1/2 teaspoon of ground coriander

Salt and black pepper, to taste

Vegetable oil for sautéing

For the Rice:

1 cup of white rice

2 cups of water

1 teaspoon of vegetable oil

1/2 teaspoon of salt

For the Protein:

1 pound of protein of your choice (commonly, chicken, beef, or fish), cooked and sliced

2 cloves of garlic, minced

Juice of 1-2 limes

Salt and black pepper, to taste

For the Plantains:

2 ripe plantains

Vegetable oil for frying

For the Salad:

2 cups of shredded cabbage or lettuce

1 tomato, sliced

1 small cucumber, sliced

1/2 red onion, thinly sliced

Fresh cilantro leaves, chopped

Lime wedges

For the Salsa Lizano:

Salsa Lizano is a popular Costa Rican condiment. If unavailable, you can use Worcestershire sauce as a substitute.

DIRECTIONS

1. **Prepare the Black Beans:**
   - In a medium saucepan, heat some vegetable oil over medium heat.
   - Add the chopped onion, minced garlic, and red bell pepper. Sauté for 2-3 minutes until they soften and become fragrant.
   - Add the black beans, ground cumin, ground coriander, salt, and black pepper.
   - Simmer for about 10-15 minutes, allowing the flavors to meld. If the beans become too dry, you can add a little water.

2. Cook the Rice:

- Rinse the white rice under cold water until the water runs clear.
- In a pot, combine the rice, water, vegetable oil, and salt.
- Bring to a boil, then reduce the heat, cover, and simmer for about 15-20 minutes, or until the rice is cooked and the water is absorbed.

3. **Prepare the Protein:**

- Season the protein (chicken, beef, or fish) with minced garlic, lime juice, salt, and black pepper.
- Cook the protein using your preferred method (grill, pan-fry, or bake), and then slice it.

4. Fry the Plantains:

- Peel and slice the ripe plantains.
- In a skillet, heat vegetable oil over medium-high heat.
- Fry the plantain slices until they are golden and caramelized on both sides.

5. Assemble the Salad:

- In a bowl, combine the shredded cabbage or lettuce, tomato slices, cucumber slices, red onion, and chopped cilantro.
- Serve with lime wedges.

6. Serve the Casado:

- To serve, arrange a portion of black beans, rice, sliced protein, fried plantains, and salad on each plate.
- Offer Salsa Lizano or Worcestershire sauce on the side for drizzling, as well as lime wedges.

Costa Rican Casado is a classic and satisfying meal that offers a delightful combination of flavors and textures. It's a popular dish in Costa Rica and a must-try if you're looking to experience the country's cuisine. Enjoy!

Olla de Carne

Serves: 6-8 Prep time: 30 min Cook time: 3 hrs

INGREDIENTS

For the Beef Broth:

2 pounds of beef shank or stewing beef

8 cups of water

1 onion, chopped

3 cloves of garlic, minced

2 carrots, chopped

2 celery stalks, chopped

1 green bell pepper, chopped

2-3 sprigs of fresh cilantro

1 teaspoon of ground cumin

Salt and black pepper, to taste

For the Soup:

1 cup of white rice

2 cups of yam or sweet potato, peeled and diced

1 cup of cassava (yuca), peeled and diced

1 cup of plantains, peeled and sliced

1 cup of corn on the cob, cut into 1-inch pieces

1/2 cup of green beans, chopped

1/2 cup of diced pumpkin or squash

1/2 cup of cabbage, chopped

1/2 cup of fresh green cilantro, chopped

1/4 cup of Salsa Lizano (a popular Costa Rican condiment, can be substituted with Worcestershire sauce)

Lime wedges, for serving

DIRECTIONS

1. **Prepare the Beef Broth:**
   - In a large pot, combine the beef shank or stewing beef with 8 cups of water.
   - Bring it to a boil, then reduce the heat to a simmer.
   - Add the chopped onion, minced garlic, carrots, celery, green bell pepper, cilantro, ground cumin, salt, and black pepper.
   - Simmer for about 1-2 hours, or until the meat is tender and the broth is rich in flavor.
   - Skim off any foam or impurities that rise to the surface.
2. **Cook the Rice:**
   - In a separate pot, cook the white rice according to the package instructions and set it aside.

3. **Prepare the Soup Ingredients:**
    - Peel and dice the yam or sweet potato, peel and dice the cassava (yuca), peel and slice the plantains, cut the corn on the cob into 1-inch pieces, chop the green beans, dice the pumpkin or squash, and chop the cabbage.
    - Prepare these ingredients to be added to the broth.
4. **Add Soup Ingredients:**
    - Once the beef is tender, add the prepared yam or sweet potato, cassava, plantains, corn, green beans, pumpkin or squash, and cabbage to the pot.
    - Simmer for another 30-45 minutes, or until the vegetables are cooked and tender.
5. **Serve:**
    - To serve, place a scoop of white rice in each serving bowl.
    - Ladle the beef, vegetables, and broth over the rice.
    - Drizzle Salsa Lizano (or Worcestershire sauce) over the top.
    - Garnish with fresh chopped cilantro and serve with lime wedges.

Costa Rican Olla de Carne is a hearty and flavorful soup that showcases the rich and diverse ingredients of the region. It's a traditional and satisfying dish, perfect for a comforting meal. Enjoy!

Picadillo

Serves: 4-6   Prep time: 15 min   Cook time: 30 min

INGREDIENTS

1 pound ground beef

1 tablespoon vegetable oil

1 onion, finely chopped

2 cloves garlic, minced

1 red bell pepper, diced

1 green bell pepper, diced

2 carrots, peeled and diced

1 potato, peeled and diced

1 cup diced tomatoes (fresh or canned)

1/2 cup beef or vegetable broth

1 teaspoon ground cumin

1 teaspoon paprika

1/2 teaspoon ground cinnamon

Salt and pepper to taste

1/4 cup chopped cilantro (optional, for garnish)

DIRECTIONS

1. **Brown the Ground Beef:**
   - In a large skillet or frying pan, heat the vegetable oil over medium-high heat.
   - Add the ground beef, breaking it up with a spatula, and cook until browned. Remove excess fat if needed.
2. **Saute the Aromatics:**
   - Add the chopped onion and minced garlic to the skillet with the browned beef. Cook until the onions turn translucent, for about 2-3 minutes.
3. **Add Vegetables and Spices:**
   - Stir in the diced red and green bell peppers, carrots, and potatoes. Cook for an additional 5 minutes until the vegetables start to soften.
   - Add the diced tomatoes and beef or vegetable broth to the skillet, combining everything well.
   - Sprinkle in ground cumin, paprika, ground cinnamon, salt, and pepper. Mix thoroughly.
4. **Simmer the Picadillo:**
   - Lower the heat to medium-low, cover the skillet, and let the mixture simmer for about 15-20 minutes or until the vegetables are tender and the flavors meld together. Stir occasionally.
5. **Serve:**
   - Once cooked, taste the picadillo and adjust seasoning if necessary.
   - Garnish with chopped cilantro if desired before serving.
   - Costa Rican Picadillo is often served with white rice, black beans, tortillas, or as a filling for empanadas.

This hearty and flavorful Costa Rican Picadillo brings together a beautiful combination of beef, vegetables, and spices, creating a delicious and comforting meal. Enjoy your homemade Picadillo!

Chorreadas

Serves: 4-6 Prep time: 10 min Cook time: 15 min

INGREDIENTS

2 cups of fresh corn kernels (about 4-5 ears of corn) or 2 cups of frozen corn, thawed

1/2 cup of all-purpose flour

1/2 cup of milk

1/4 cup of sugar

2 eggs

2 tablespoons of butter, melted

1/2 teaspoon of salt

1/4 teaspoon of black pepper

Vegetable oil for cooking

Sour cream, for serving (optional)

Fresh cilantro leaves, for garnish (optional)

DIRECTIONS

1. **Prepare the Corn:**
   - If using fresh corn, remove the kernels from the cobs. You can do this with a knife or a corn stripper tool.
   - If using frozen corn, make sure it's thawed.
2. **Blend the Corn:**
   - Place the corn kernels in a blender or food processor and blend until you have a smooth corn puree.
3. **Mix the Batter:**
   - In a mixing bowl, combine the corn puree with the all-purpose flour, milk, sugar, eggs, melted butter, salt, and black pepper.
   - Stir until all the ingredients are well incorporated, creating a smooth batter.
4. **Cook the Chorreadas:**
   - In a large skillet, heat a small amount of vegetable oil over medium heat.
   - Pour a portion of the batter (about 1/4 cup) into the skillet for each chorreada.
   - Cook until bubbles form on the surface, then flip and cook the other side until they are golden brown and cooked through, about 2-3 minutes per side.
   - Continue this process until you've used all the batter. You may need to add more oil to the skillet as you go.
5. **Serve:**
   - Serve the Costa Rican Chorreadas hot, either as a side dish or as a breakfast item.
   - They can be enjoyed with a dollop of sour cream and garnished with fresh cilantro leaves if desired.

Costa Rican Chorreadas are a delicious and versatile dish that can be served for breakfast, as a side, or as a snack. The combination of fresh corn and a touch of sweetness makes them a delightful addition to your Costa Rican culinary experience. Enjoy!

Ceviche

Serves: 4-6   Prep time: 20 min   Cook time: N/A

INGREDIENTS

For the Ceviche:

1 pound of fresh white fish (such as sea bass, snapper, or tilapia), cut into small cubes

1 cup of fresh lime juice (from about 12-15 limes)

1/2 cup of finely chopped red onion

1/2 cup of finely chopped bell pepper (any color)

1/4 cup of finely chopped fresh cilantro

1-2 cloves of garlic, minced

1-2 small chili peppers (jalapeño, serrano, or similar), seeded and minced (adjust to your desired level of spiciness)

1 teaspoon of salt

1/4 teaspoon of black pepper

1/4 teaspoon of ground cumin

1/4 teaspoon of paprika

1/4 teaspoon of dried oregano

1/4 cup of tomato ketchup

1/4 cup of tomato juice (optional)

1/4 cup of Clamato juice (optional)

Ice cubes (optional)

For Serving:

Tortilla chips or saltine crackers

Sliced avocado (optional)

Lime wedges

Hot sauce (optional)

DIRECTIONS

1. **Prepare the Fish:**
   - Cut the fresh white fish into small, bite-sized cubes. Make sure they are uniform in size.
2. **Marinate the Fish:**
   - In a large glass or non-metallic bowl, place the fish cubes.
   - Pour the fresh lime juice over the fish, ensuring that it's completely submerged. The acid in the lime juice will "cook" the fish. Cover and refrigerate for about 1-2 hours until the fish turns opaque and "cooked."
3. **Prepare the Aromatics:**
   - In a separate bowl, combine the finely chopped red onion, bell pepper, cilantro, minced garlic, and minced chili peppers.
4. **Mix the Ceviche:**
   - Once the fish is "cooked," drain most of the lime juice from the bowl.
   - Add the prepared aromatics to the fish.
5. **Season the Ceviche:**
   - Add the salt, black pepper, ground cumin, paprika, dried oregano, tomato ketchup, and tomato juice (if using).
   - Gently stir to combine all the ingredients. Taste and adjust the seasonings as needed. If you prefer a spicier ceviche, you can add more minced chili peppers.

6. **Chill the Ceviche:**

- Cover the ceviche and refrigerate for an additional 15-30 minutes to let the flavors meld.

7. Serve:

- Serve the Costa Rican Ceviche in individual bowls or on a platter.
- Offer tortilla chips or saltine crackers for scooping.
- Optionally, garnish with sliced avocado, lime wedges, and hot sauce on the side.

Costa Rican Ceviche is a refreshing and zesty dish that showcases the vibrant flavors of the region. It's perfect as an appetizer or a light meal, especially on a hot day. Enjoy!

Pozole

Serves: 6-8 Prep time: 15 min Cook time: 3hrs

INGREDIENTS

2 cups dried hominy (maíz mote pelado)

1 pound pork shoulder or pork butt, cubed

1 onion, chopped

3 cloves garlic, minced

2 tablespoons vegetable oil

1 teaspoon dried oregano

1 teaspoon ground cumin

1 teaspoon ground coriander

Salt and pepper to taste

6 cups chicken or vegetable broth

Garnishes: shredded cabbage, sliced radishes, chopped cilantro, lime wedges, diced onion

DIRECTIONS

1. **Prepare the Hominy:**
   - Soak the dried hominy in water overnight or for at least 8 hours. Drain and rinse thoroughly.
2. **Brown the Pork:**
   - In a large pot or Dutch oven, heat the vegetable oil over medium-high heat. Add the cubed pork and brown it on all sides, about 5-7 minutes.
3. **Cook Aromatics:**
   - Add the chopped onion and minced garlic to the pot with the pork. Sauté until the onion turns translucent, about 3-4 minutes.
4. **Season and Simmer:**
   - Stir in the dried oregano, ground cumin, ground coriander, salt, and pepper. Cook for an additional minute to toast the spices.
   - Add the soaked hominy to the pot and pour in the chicken or vegetable broth.
   - Bring the mixture to a boil, then reduce the heat to low, cover, and simmer for 2-3 hours or until the pork is tender and the hominy is fully cooked. Stir occasionally and add more broth or water if needed.
5. **Adjust Seasoning:**
   - Taste and adjust the seasoning with additional salt and pepper if necessary.
6. **Serve:**
   - Ladle the Pozole into bowls.
   - Serve the Pozole hot, allowing everyone to garnish their bowls with shredded cabbage, sliced radishes, chopped cilantro, lime wedges, and diced onion according to their preferences.
7. **Enjoy:**
   - Enjoy the comforting and flavorful Costa Rican Pozole as a complete meal on its own or accompanied by warm tortillas or bread.

This Pozole recipe can be customized by adding other vegetables like carrots or bell peppers. It's a delicious and warming dish, perfect for gatherings or family meals. Adjust the spices and garnishes to suit your taste.

Section 3

El Salvador

Pupusas

Serves: 6-8 Prep time: 30 min Cook time: 20 min

INGREDIENTS

For the Pupusa Dough:

2 cups of masa harina (corn flour)

1 1/2 cups of warm water

1/2 teaspoon of salt

For the Pupusa Filling (choose one or more):

1 1/2 cups of shredded cheese (quesillo or mozzarella)

1 1/2 cups of refried beans (frijoles refritos)

1/2 cup of cooked and seasoned ground pork (chicharrón molido)

1/2 cup of cooked and seasoned shredded chicken

1/2 cup of loroco flowers (a Salvadoran edible flower) or other vegetables, finely chopped

For the Curtido (Cabbage Slaw):

2 cups of finely shredded cabbage

1/2 cup of finely chopped white onion

1/2 cup of finely chopped carrot

1/4 cup of chopped fresh oregano leaves (substitute with dried oregano if needed)

1/2 cup of white vinegar

1/2 cup of water

1/2 teaspoon of red pepper flakes

Salt and black pepper, to taste

For the Salsa Roja (Red Sauce):

3 ripe tomatoes

1/2 white onion

2 cloves of garlic

1 jalapeño pepper (adjust to your desired level of spiciness)

Fresh cilantro leaves

Salt and black pepper, to taste

DIRECTIONS

1. **Prepare the Pupusa Dough:**
   - In a large mixing bowl, combine the masa harina and salt.
   - Slowly add the warm water while kneading the dough with your hands until it's smooth and pliable.
   - If the dough is too dry, add a little more water; if it's too sticky, add a bit more masa harina.
   - Cover the dough and let it rest for 10-15 minutes.
2. **Prepare the Curtido (Cabbage Slaw):**
   - In a bowl, combine the shredded cabbage, chopped white onion, chopped carrot, fresh oregano, white vinegar, water, red pepper flakes, salt, and black pepper.
   - Mix well, cover, and refrigerate for at least 30 minutes, allowing the flavors to meld.
3. **Prepare the Salsa Roja (Red Sauce):**
   - In a blender or food processor, combine the ripe tomatoes, white onion, garlic, jalapeño pepper, fresh cilantro leaves, salt, and black pepper.
   - Blend until smooth. Adjust the spiciness by adding more or fewer jalapeño peppers.

4. **Assemble the Pupusas:**
   - Take a small handful of pupusa dough and roll it into a ball (about the size of a golf ball).
   - Make an indentation in the center and add your choice of filling, such as cheese, refried beans, seasoned ground pork, shredded chicken, or loroco flowers.
   - Close the dough around the filling, creating a thick disc. Flatten it with your hands to about 1/4-inch thickness, ensuring the filling is evenly distributed.
5. **Cook the Pupusas:**
   - Heat a griddle or skillet over medium-high heat.
   - Place the pupusas on the hot griddle and cook for about 3-4 minutes on each side until they develop a golden-brown crust.
   - Remove from the griddle and keep warm.
6. **Serve:**
   - Serve the El Salvador Pupusas hot, accompanied by curtido and salsa roja on the side. Enjoy!

El Salvador Pupusas are a beloved and traditional Central American dish that can be filled with various ingredients to suit your taste. The combination of pupusas, curtido, and salsa roja is a delicious and satisfying meal.

Pan con Pollo

Serves: 4 Prep time: 15 min Cook time: 30 min

INGREDIENTS

For the Chicken:

1 pound boneless, skinless chicken breasts or thighs

1 onion, finely chopped

2 cloves garlic, minced

1 bell pepper, diced

1 tomato, diced

1 teaspoon ground cumin

1 teaspoon dried oregano

Salt and pepper to taste

2 tablespoons vegetable oil

2 cups chicken broth or water

For the Sandwich:

Bolillo rolls or French bread, sliced lengthwise

Mayonnaise

Sliced tomatoes

Sliced onions

Lettuce leaves

Optional: avocado slices, hot sauce

DIRECTIONS

1. **Cook the Chicken:**
   - Cut the chicken into small pieces.
   - In a skillet or pot, heat the vegetable oil over medium-high heat.
   - Add the chopped onions, garlic, bell pepper, and tomato. Sauté until the vegetables soften.
   - Add the chicken pieces, cumin, oregano, salt, and pepper. Cook until the chicken is browned on all sides.
   - Pour in the chicken broth or water. Bring to a boil, then reduce the heat and let it simmer until the chicken is fully cooked and tender. This will take around 15-20 minutes.
2. **Assemble the Sandwiches:**
   - Slice the bolillo rolls or French bread lengthwise.
   - Spread a layer of mayonnaise on the bottom half of each roll.
   - Add a generous portion of the cooked chicken and vegetables on top of the mayo.
   - Layer with sliced tomatoes, onions, lettuce, and any optional ingredients like avocado slices or hot sauce.
   - Top each sandwich with the other half of the roll.
3. **Serve:**
   - Pan con Pollo is often served with a side of coleslaw, potato chips, or pickled vegetables.
   - Serve immediately while the bread is still fresh and warm.

This recipe offers a tasty way to enjoy the flavors of seasoned chicken and vegetables nestled within crusty bread. Adjust the fillings and toppings according to personal preferences. Enjoy your Pan con Pollo!

Atol de Elote

Serves: 4-6 Prep time: 10 min Cook time: 40 min

INGREDIENTS

2 cups of fresh corn kernels (you can use corn on the cob and cut the kernels off or use frozen corn)

4 cups of whole milk

1/2 cup of sugar (adjust to your desired sweetness)

1/2 cup of masa harina (corn flour)

1 cinnamon stick

2-3 whole cloves (optional)

1/4 teaspoon of ground cinnamon (for garnish)

1/4 teaspoon of ground nutmeg (for garnish)

1/4 teaspoon of vanilla extract (optional)

Pinch of salt

DIRECTIONS

1. **Prepare the Corn:**
   - If using fresh corn on the cob, cut the kernels off the cob. You should have about 2 cups of corn kernels.
   - If using frozen corn, make sure it's thawed.
2. **Blend the Corn:**
   - Place the corn kernels and 2 cups of milk in a blender or food processor.
   - Blend until you have a smooth corn puree.
3. **Prepare the Atole Base:**
   - In a large saucepan, combine the remaining 2 cups of milk, sugar, masa harina, cinnamon stick, and whole cloves (if using).
   - Stir well to combine all the ingredients.
4. **Cook the Atole:**
   - Heat the mixture over medium heat, stirring constantly to prevent lumps from forming.
   - Continue to cook and stir for about 10-15 minutes, or until the mixture thickens.
5. **Add the Corn Puree:**
   - Pour the corn puree into the saucepan with the atole base.
   - Stir well to combine.
6. **Add Flavorings:**
   - If desired, add a pinch of salt and a few drops of vanilla extract for extra flavor.
7. **Continue Cooking:**
   - Cook the atole over low heat for an additional 10-15 minutes, stirring constantly to prevent sticking.
8. **Serve:**
   - Remove the cinnamon stick and whole cloves (if used).
   - Ladle the El Salvador Corn Atole into serving mugs or bowls.
9. **Garnish:**
   - Sprinkle a pinch of ground cinnamon and ground nutmeg on top of each serving for a touch of flavor and decoration.

10. **Serve Hot:**

- Serve the corn atole hot. It's a comforting and traditional Salvadoran drink often enjoyed during breakfast or as a sweet snack.

El Salvador Corn Atole is a delightful and creamy corn-based drink that offers a warm and comforting experience. It's a popular beverage in Salvadoran cuisine, perfect for enjoying on a chilly day or as a sweet treat.

Torrejas

Serves: 4-6 Prep time: 20 min Cook time: 25 min

INGREDIENTS

For the Torrejas:

4-6 slices of stale bread (French bread or any bread of your choice)

2 cups of whole milk

2 eggs

1/2 cup of sugar

1 teaspoon of ground cinnamon

1/2 teaspoon of vanilla extract

Vegetable oil, for frying

For the Sugar Syrup:

1 cup of water

1 cup of brown sugar

2-3 whole cloves

1 cinnamon stick

DIRECTIONS

1. **Prepare the Sugar Syrup:**
   - In a saucepan, combine the water, brown sugar, whole cloves, and cinnamon stick.
   - Bring the mixture to a boil, then reduce the heat and let it simmer for about 10-15 minutes until it thickens into a syrup.
   - Remove the saucepan from heat and set aside to cool. Once cooled, remove the cloves and cinnamon stick.
2. **Soak the Bread Slices:**
   - In a shallow dish, soak the stale bread slices in the whole milk for about 5-10 minutes. Make sure they absorb the milk.
3. **Beat the Eggs:**
   - In a separate bowl, beat the eggs.
4. **Prepare the Torrejas Mixture:**
   - In a mixing bowl, combine the soaked bread slices, beaten eggs, sugar, ground cinnamon, and vanilla extract.
   - Mix well to create a thick and creamy mixture.
5. **Fry the Torrejas:**
   - In a large skillet or frying pan, heat vegetable oil over medium-high heat.
   - Take a portion of the torrejas mixture and form it into a patty.
   - Carefully place the patty in the hot oil and fry until golden brown on both sides, about 2-3 minutes per side.
   - Continue this process until all the torrejas are cooked.
   - Place the fried torrejas on paper towels to remove excess oil.
6. **Serve with Sugar Syrup:**
   - To serve, drizzle the prepared sugar syrup over the torrejas while they're still warm.
   - Enjoy your El Salvador Torrejas as a sweet and delicious treat!

El Salvador Torrejas are a traditional and beloved dessert in Salvadoran cuisine. They are sweet and flavorful, making them perfect for a special occasion or as a delightful sweet indulgence.

Tamales Pisque

Serves: 6-8 Prep time: 30 min Cook time: 3 hrs

INGREDIENTS

For the Tamal Dough:

2 cups of masa harina (corn flour)

1/4 cup of vegetable oil

3 cups of warm water

1 teaspoon of salt

For the Filling (Pisque):

1 cup of red or black beans (cooked and drained)

1/2 cup of grated queso duro or queso fresco (hard or fresh cheese)

1/4 cup of minced pork (cooked)

1/4 cup of tomato sauce

1/4 cup of cooked and diced green bell pepper

1/4 cup of cooked and diced onion

2 cloves of garlic, minced

1 teaspoon of ground cumin

1/2 teaspoon of dried oregano

Salt and black pepper, to taste

For Wrapping:

Banana leaves or aluminum foil

DIRECTIONS

1. **Prepare the Filling (Pisque):**
   - In a large skillet, heat a bit of vegetable oil over medium heat.
   - Add the minced pork and cook until it's browned and cooked through.
   - Add the cooked and drained beans, grated cheese, tomato sauce, cooked green bell pepper, diced onion, minced garlic, ground cumin, dried oregano, salt, and black pepper.
   - Cook and stir the mixture until it's well combined and heated through. Set the pisque mixture aside.
2. **Prepare the Tamal Dough:**
   - In a mixing bowl, combine the masa harina, vegetable oil, warm water, and salt.
   - Knead the dough until it's smooth and pliable.
3. **Assemble the Tamales:**
   - Place a banana leaf or aluminum foil sheet on a clean surface.
   - Take a portion of the tamal dough and form it into a small disc on the banana leaf or foil.
   - Add a spoonful of the prepared pisque filling in the center of the dough.
4. **Wrap the Tamales:**
   - Fold the banana leaf or foil over the tamal, making sure to enclose the filling completely.
   - Secure the tamal with kitchen twine or string.
5. **Steam the Tamales:**
   - Place the tamales in a large steamer or pot.
   - Steam the tamales over boiling water for about 1.5 to 2 hours, or until the tamal dough is fully cooked and the tamales have set.

6. Serve:

- Allow the tamales to cool slightly before serving.
- Unwrap and serve your El Salvador Tamal Pisque while they're still warm.

Tamal Pisque is a traditional and flavorful dish from El Salvador that combines the rich texture of tamal dough with a delicious bean and cheese filling. It's a delightful treat and a popular dish for special occasions and gatherings. Enjoy!

Yuca Sancochada

Serves: 6-8 Prep time: 20 min Cook time: 40 min

INGREDIENTS

2 pounds of yuca (cassava), peeled and cut into large chunks

2-3 cloves of garlic, minced

1 onion, chopped

2 tomatoes, chopped

1 bell pepper (any color), chopped

1/2 cup of fresh cilantro leaves, chopped

2 tablespoons of vegetable oil

6 cups of water

2 teaspoons of salt (adjust to taste)

1/2 teaspoon of black pepper

1/2 teaspoon of ground cumin

1/2 teaspoon of dried oregano

1 bay leaf

Lime wedges, for serving

DIRECTIONS

1. **Prepare the Yuca:**
   - Start by peeling the yuca and cutting it into large, manageable chunks. Be sure to remove any woody or fibrous centers.
   - Rinse the yuca under cold water.
2. **Sauté Aromatics:**
   - In a large pot, heat the vegetable oil over medium heat.
   - Add the minced garlic, chopped onion, chopped tomatoes, and chopped bell pepper.
   - Sauté the aromatics until they become soft and fragrant, about 5 minutes.
3. **Add Seasonings:**
   - Add the salt, black pepper, ground cumin, dried oregano, and bay leaf to the pot.
   - Stir well to distribute the seasonings evenly.
4. **Cook the Yuca:**
   - Add the yuca chunks to the pot, followed by 6 cups of water.
   - Bring the mixture to a boil and then reduce the heat to a simmer.
   - Cook the yuca for about 20-30 minutes, or until it becomes tender and can be easily pierced with a fork.
5. **Add Cilantro:**
   - In the last 5 minutes of cooking, stir in the chopped cilantro leaves.
6. **Serve:**
   - Remove the bay leaf from the pot.
   - Serve the El Salvador Yuca Sancochada hot, garnished with lime wedges on the side.

El Salvador Yuca Sancochada is a delightful and flavorful dish that showcases the rich and starchy yuca paired with aromatic seasonings. It's a traditional and comforting Salvadoran recipe, perfect for a hearty meal. Enjoy!

Pastelitos

Serves: 4-6 Prep time: 30 min Cook time: 25 min

INGREDIENTS

For the Dough:

2 cups of masa harina (corn flour)

1 1/2 cups of warm water

1/4 cup of vegetable oil

1/2 teaspoon of salt

For the Filling:

1/2 pound of ground pork or beef

1/2 cup of finely chopped onion

1/4 cup of finely chopped bell pepper (any color)

2 cloves of garlic, minced

1/2 teaspoon of ground cumin

1/2 teaspoon of dried oregano

Salt and black pepper, to taste

Vegetable oil for frying

For the Curtido (Cabbage Slaw):

3 cups of finely shredded cabbage

1/2 cup of finely chopped white onion

1/2 cup of finely chopped carrot

1/4 cup of chopped fresh oregano leaves (substitute with dried oregano if needed)

1/2 cup of white vinegar

1/2 cup of water

1/2 teaspoon of red pepper flakes

Salt and black pepper, to taste

DIRECTIONS

1. **Prepare the Dough:**
   - In a mixing bowl, combine the masa harina and salt.
   - Slowly add the warm water and vegetable oil, and knead the dough until it's smooth and pliable.
   - Cover the dough and let it rest for about 10-15 minutes.
2. **Prepare the Filling:**
   - In a skillet, heat a bit of vegetable oil over medium heat.
   - Add the ground pork or beef and cook until browned and cooked through.
   - Add the chopped onion, bell pepper, minced garlic, ground cumin, dried oregano, salt, and black pepper.
   - Cook and stir the mixture until the vegetables are tender and the flavors meld. Set the filling aside.
3. **Prepare the Curtido (Cabbage Slaw):**
   - In a bowl, combine the shredded cabbage, chopped white onion, chopped carrot, fresh oregano, white vinegar, water, red pepper flakes, salt, and black pepper.
   - Mix well, cover, and refrigerate for at least 30 minutes to let the flavors meld.

4. **Assemble the Pastelitos:**
   - Take a small portion of the masa dough and form it into a ball (about the size of a golf ball).
   - Flatten the dough into a disc on a clean surface, creating a small pocket.
5. **Add the Filling:**
   - Place a spoonful of the prepared filling into the center of the masa dough.
6. **Fold and Seal:**
   - Carefully fold the dough over the filling, creating a half-moon shape.
   - Seal the edges by pressing them together to enclose the filling completely.
7. **Fry the Pastelitos:**
   - In a large skillet or frying pan, heat vegetable oil over medium-high heat.
   - Carefully place the pastelitos in the hot oil and fry until they are golden brown on both sides, about 2-3 minutes per side.
   - Remove from the oil and place on paper towels to drain excess oil.
8. **Serve with Curtido:**
   - Serve the El Salvador Pastelitos hot, accompanied by curtido on the side.

El Salvador Pastelitos are a delicious and savory snack that combines the richness of masa dough with a flavorful meat filling. They are typically enjoyed with curtido, a tangy cabbage slaw. Enjoy!

Sopa de Pata

Serves: 6-8 Prep time: 30 min Cook time: 3 hrs

INGREDIENTS

2 pounds of cow's feet (pata de res), cleaned and split into manageable pieces

1/2 cup of long-grain rice

1/2 cup of white corn kernels (hominy)

1/2 cup of peeled and cubed cassava (yuca)

1/2 cup of peeled and cubed green plantains

1/2 cup of peeled and cubed sweet potatoes

1/2 cup of chopped white onion

3 cloves of garlic, minced

2 tomatoes, chopped

1 green bell pepper, chopped

1/2 cup of chopped fresh cilantro leaves

1 teaspoon of ground cumin

1/2 teaspoon of dried oregano

1/4 teaspoon of ground achiote (annatto) for color (optional)

Salt and black pepper, to taste

Vegetable oil for sautéing

Lime wedges, for serving

DIRECTIONS

1. **Clean and Prepare the Cow's Feet:**
   - In a large pot, place the cow's feet and cover them with water.
   - Bring the water to a boil and let it boil for about 10 minutes.
   - Drain the water and rinse the cow's feet thoroughly. This helps remove any impurities.
2. **Boil the Cow's Feet:**
   - Return the cow's feet to the pot and cover them with fresh water.
   - Bring the water to a boil, reduce the heat to a simmer, and cook the cow's feet for about 1.5-2 hours, or until they become tender.
   - Skim any impurities that rise to the surface during cooking.
3. **Sauté Aromatics:**
   - In a separate skillet, heat some vegetable oil over medium heat.
   - Add the chopped onion, minced garlic, chopped tomatoes, and chopped green bell pepper.
   - Sauté the aromatics until they become soft and fragrant, about 5-7 minutes.
4. **Prepare Vegetables:**
   - In a large pot, combine the cooked cow's feet, sautéed aromatics, long-grain rice, white corn kernels (hominy), cubed cassava, cubed green plantains, and cubed sweet potatoes.
5. **Add Seasonings:**
   - Stir in the ground cumin, dried oregano, and ground achiote (if using) for color.
   - Season with salt and black pepper to taste.

6. Cook the Soup:

- Add enough water to the pot to cover all the ingredients.
- Bring the soup to a boil, then reduce the heat to a simmer.
- Cook for another 30-40 minutes, or until all the vegetables are tender and the flavors meld together.
- Adjust the seasoning if needed.

7. Serve:

- Serve El Salvador Leg Soup (Sopa de Pata) hot, garnished with fresh cilantro leaves and lime wedges on the side.

El Salvador Leg Soup, or Sopa de Pata, is a hearty and flavorful soup featuring cow's feet and an array of vegetables and seasonings. It's a beloved traditional Salvadoran dish that is perfect for a warming and satisfying meal. Enjoy!

Nuegados

Serves: 12pcs Prep time: 20 min Cook time: 20 min

INGREDIENTS

2 cups grated cassava or yuca (fresh or frozen, make sure it's well-drained)

1/2 cup all-purpose flour

1/4 cup sugar

1/4 teaspoon salt

1/4 teaspoon ground cinnamon

Vegetable oil for frying

For the Syrup (optional):

1 cup water

1 cup brown sugar

2 cinnamon sticks

2 whole cloves

DIRECTIONS

1. **Prepare the Dough:**
    - In a mixing bowl, combine the grated cassava, flour, sugar, salt, and ground cinnamon. Mix well until a smooth dough forms. If the mixture is too dry, you can add a tablespoon of water at a time to moisten it slightly.
2. **Shape the Nuegados:**
    - Take small portions of the dough and roll them into balls, about the size of a walnut. Flatten them slightly to form discs. You can shape them as you prefer, either round or oval.
3. **Fry the Nuegados:**
    - In a deep skillet or frying pan, heat vegetable oil over medium heat.
    - Carefully place the shaped nuegados into the hot oil. Fry them in batches, making sure not to overcrowd the pan.
    - Fry each side until they turn golden brown, which should take about 3-4 minutes per side.
    - Remove the fried nuegados from the oil and place them on paper towels to drain any excess oil.
4. **Make the Syrup (Optional):**
    - If you'd like to add a syrupy coating to the nuegados, combine water, brown sugar, cinnamon sticks, and cloves in a saucepan.
    - Bring the mixture to a boil, then reduce the heat and simmer for about 5-7 minutes until it thickens slightly.
    - Remove from heat and let it cool for a few minutes.
5. **Coat the Nuegados (Optional):**
    - Dip the fried nuegados into the syrup one at a time, coating them evenly.
    - Place the coated nuegados on a wire rack or a plate to allow the excess syrup to drip off.
6. **Serve:**
    - Nuegados can be served warm or at room temperature. They're delightful on their own or paired with a cup of coffee or hot chocolate.

This recipe for Nuegados offers a delightful taste of Salvadoran cuisine. The sweet, fried goodness of these treats is sure to be a hit! Adjust the sweetness by modifying the syrup or dust them with powdered sugar instead. Enjoy your homemade Nuegados!

Tortillas

Serves: 13pcs Prep time: 15 min Cook time: 15 min

INGREDIENTS

2 cups of masa harina (corn flour)

1 1/2 cups of warm water

1/2 teaspoon of salt (optional)

DIRECTIONS

1. **Prepare the Masa Dough:**
   - In a mixing bowl, combine the masa harina and salt (if using).
   - Gradually add the warm water while kneading the dough until it's smooth and pliable. The dough should be moist but not sticky. You may need to adjust the water or masa harina to achieve the right consistency.
2. **Let the Dough Rest:**
   - Cover the dough with a clean cloth or plastic wrap and let it rest for about 15-20 minutes. This resting period allows the masa to fully hydrate.

3. **Preheat a Griddle or Comal:**

- While the dough is resting, preheat a griddle or comal over medium-high heat. A cast-iron skillet can also be used if you don't have a comal.

4. **Form the Tortillas:**

- Take a small portion of the masa dough, about the size of a golf ball, and roll it into a ball.
- Place the ball between two sheets of plastic wrap or parchment paper.

5. **Flatten the Tortillas:**

- Using a tortilla press or a flat, heavy object (like the bottom of a heavy skillet), press the ball of dough to flatten it into a round tortilla. Aim for a thickness of about 1/8 inch.

6. **Cook the Tortillas:**

- Carefully peel the flattened dough off the plastic wrap and place it on the hot griddle or comal.
- Cook the tortilla for about 1-2 minutes on each side or until it begins to puff up slightly and shows some brown spots.
- You can press down gently on the tortilla with a spatula to help it puff.

7. **Keep Warm:**

- As each tortilla is cooked, transfer it to a clean kitchen towel and fold the towel over to keep the tortillas warm and soft.

8. **Serve:**

- Serve the freshly made Salvadoran corn tortillas as a side to your favorite Salvadoran dishes, such as pupusas, tamales, or as a base for various toppings like refried beans and cheese.

Salvadoran corn tortillas are a staple in Salvadoran cuisine and serve as the foundation for many traditional dishes. They are delicious, gluten-free, and easy to make at home. Enjoy!

Chimol

Serves: 4-6   Prep time: 15 min   Cook time: N/A

INGREDIENTS

4 ripe tomatoes, finely diced

1/2 onion, finely chopped

1/2 cup fresh cilantro, chopped

1-2 jalapeño or serrano peppers, finely chopped (adjust to preferred spiciness)

Juice of 2-3 limes

Salt to taste

DIRECTIONS

1. **Prepare the Ingredients:**
    - Finely dice the tomatoes, ensuring to remove the seeds and excess moisture.
    - Chop the onion, cilantro, and peppers finely. Remove the seeds and membrane from the peppers if you prefer less heat.

2. **Mix the Chimol:**
   - In a mixing bowl, combine the diced tomatoes, chopped onions, cilantro, and jalapeño or serrano peppers.
   - Squeeze the lime juice over the mixture. Start with the juice of 2 limes and adjust based on taste preference.
   - Season with salt to taste.
3. **Let it Rest:**
   - Gently toss all the ingredients together until well combined.
   - Allow the chimol to rest for at least 10-15 minutes before serving. This allows the flavors to meld together.
4. **Serve:**
   - Chimol is typically served as a side dish or condiment alongside various Salvadoran dishes, such as pupusas, grilled meats, or as a topping for tacos and other Central American dishes.

This fresh and zesty salsa adds a burst of flavor to any dish. Adjust the amount of lime and jalapeño/serrano peppers according to your taste preferences. Enjoy your homemade Salvadoran Chimol!

Section 4

Guatemala

Pepian

Serves: 6-8   Prep time: 30 min   Cook time: 3 hrs

INGREDIENTS

For the Pepián Sauce:

1/2 cup of sesame seeds

1/4 cup of pumpkin seeds (pepitas)

1/4 cup of roasted peanuts

1/4 cup of almonds

4-6 dried guajillo chilies (or dried red chilies), seeds and stems removed

2-3 cloves of garlic

1/2 cup of chopped white onion

1/2 teaspoon of ground cinnamon

1/2 teaspoon of ground allspice

1/4 teaspoon of ground cloves

1/4 teaspoon of ground coriander

1/4 teaspoon of ground cumin

Salt and black pepper, to taste

2-3 cups of chicken or vegetable broth

2-3 tablespoons of vegetable oil

For the Stew:

2 pounds of chicken pieces (or beef, pork, or vegetables for a vegetarian option)

2-3 tablespoons of vegetable oil

2-3 cups of pepián sauce (prepared as above)

1/2 cup of white corn tortillas, toasted and ground into a paste (optional, for thickening)

1-2 potatoes, peeled and cubed

1-2 carrots, peeled and sliced

1-2 zucchinis, sliced

1-2 ears of fresh corn on the cob, cut into rounds

1/2 cup of green beans, cut into pieces

1/2 cup of fresh green peas

1-2 chayotes, peeled and cubed (optional)

1-2 pieces of güisquil (chayote squash), peeled and cubed (optional)

Salt and black pepper, to taste

DIRECTIONS

1. **Prepare the Pepián Sauce:**
   - In a dry skillet, toast the sesame seeds, pumpkin seeds, peanuts, and almonds over medium heat until they are lightly browned. Set them aside.
   - In the same skillet, toast the dried guajillo chilies until they become fragrant and slightly crispy.
   - In a blender or food processor, combine the toasted seeds and nuts, toasted chilies, garlic, chopped onion, ground cinnamon, ground allspice, ground cloves, ground coriander, ground cumin, salt, black pepper, and enough chicken or vegetable broth to create a smooth sauce.
   - Blend until the mixture is smooth and set the pepián sauce aside.

2. **Prepare the Stew:**
   - In a large pot or Dutch oven, heat the vegetable oil over medium-high heat.
   - Add the chicken pieces and brown them on all sides. If using other proteins or vegetables, brown them accordingly.
   - Once browned, remove the chicken (or other components) from the pot and set aside.
3. **Cook the Pepián:**
   - In the same pot, add the prepared pepián sauce and let it simmer over medium heat for about 5-10 minutes, stirring frequently.
   - If the sauce is too thick, you can add more chicken or vegetable broth to reach your desired consistency.
4. **Return the Chicken and Add Vegetables:**
   - Return the browned chicken pieces to the pot with the pepián sauce.
   - Add the toasted and ground tortilla paste (if using) to thicken the stew.
   - Add the potatoes, carrots, zucchinis, fresh corn rounds, green beans, green peas, chayotes, and güisquil (if using).
   - Stir well and add more chicken or vegetable broth as needed to cover the ingredients.
5. **Simmer and Cook:**
   - Cover the pot and let the stew simmer over low heat for about 1.5-2 hours, or until the chicken is cooked through, and the vegetables are tender. If using other proteins or vegetables, adjust the cooking time accordingly.
6. **Serve:**
   - Serve Guatemalan Pepián hot with a side of rice, tortillas, or crusty bread.

Guatemalan Pepián is a rich and flavorful stew with deep, aromatic notes. It's a classic and traditional dish in Guatemalan cuisine, often enjoyed on special occasions and gatherings. Enjoy your homemade Pepián!

Kak'ik

Serves: 6-8 Prep time: 30 min Cook time: 3 hrs

INGREDIENTS

1 whole turkey (about 3-4 pounds), cut into pieces (you can use parts like thighs and drumsticks)

10 cups water or chicken broth

4-5 tomatoes, chopped

2 onions, chopped

4 cloves garlic, minced

2 bell peppers (1 red, 1 green), chopped

4-5 fresh mint leaves

4-5 fresh cilantro sprigs

4-5 fresh oregano sprigs

2 tablespoons achiote paste (annatto paste)

4-5 guaque chilies (or substitute with mild dried chili peppers)

1 teaspoon ground allspice

1 teaspoon ground cumin

1 teaspoon dried oregano

Salt and pepper to taste

2-3 tablespoons vegetable oil

DIRECTIONS

1. Prepare the Turkey and Broth:
   - Rinse the turkey pieces thoroughly and pat them dry.
   - In a large pot, add the turkey pieces and cover them with water or chicken broth. Bring it to a boil.
   - Reduce the heat to low and let the turkey simmer for about 1.5 to 2 hours until it becomes tender. Skim off any foam that forms on the surface.
2. Prepare the Aromatic Base:
   - In a separate skillet, heat the vegetable oil over medium heat.
   - Add chopped onions, minced garlic, and bell peppers. Sauté until they are soft and fragrant.
   - Add the chopped tomatoes and cook until they break down and form a thick sauce.
3. Prepare the Spice Paste:
   - In a blender or mortar and pestle, combine the achiote paste, fresh mint leaves, cilantro, oregano, guaque chilies (or dried chili peppers), ground allspice, ground cumin, dried oregano, salt, and pepper. Blend or grind until it forms a smooth paste.
4. Combine Everything:
   - Add the spice paste mixture to the pot of simmering turkey along with the sautéed aromatic base. Stir well to combine.
   - Let the soup simmer for an additional 30-40 minutes to allow the flavors to meld together. Adjust seasoning if needed.
5. Serve:
   - Once ready, serve the Kak'ik hot, typically accompanied by rice and corn tortillas.

Kak'ik is a flavorful and aromatic soup that represents Guatemala's rich culinary heritage. It's often enjoyed during special occasions and celebrations. Adjust the spiciness by modifying the amount of chili peppers used. Enjoy your homemade Guatemalan Kak'ik!

Hilachas

Serves: 6-8 Prep time: 20 min Cook time: 3 hrs

INGREDIENTS

2 pounds beef (brisket or flank), cut into chunks

1 onion, finely chopped

4-5 tomatoes, chopped

4-5 cloves garlic, minced

2 bell peppers (1 red, 1 green), chopped

2 carrots, peeled and chopped

2-3 potatoes, peeled and diced

2 bay leaves

4-5 whole cloves

1 teaspoon dried oregano

1 teaspoon ground cumin

1 teaspoon paprika

Salt and pepper to taste

Vegetable oil for cooking

Chopped fresh cilantro for garnish (optional)
Cooked rice and corn tortillas for serving

DIRECTIONS

1. **Prepare the Beef:**
   - In a large pot or Dutch oven, heat some vegetable oil over medium-high heat.
   - Add the beef chunks and brown them on all sides for a few minutes.
2. **Create the Sauce Base:**
   - Once the beef is browned, add the chopped onion and minced garlic. Sauté until they become translucent and fragrant.
   - Add the chopped tomatoes and bell peppers. Cook until the tomatoes break down and release their juices, forming a thick sauce.
3. **Cook the Beef:**
   - Return the browned beef to the pot with the tomato mixture.
   - Add enough water to cover the beef. Then, add the bay leaves, whole cloves, dried oregano, ground cumin, paprika, salt, and pepper. Stir well.
   - Bring the mixture to a boil, then reduce the heat to low, cover the pot, and let it simmer for about 2-3 hours until the beef becomes tender and easily shreds.
4. **Shred the Beef:**
   - Once the beef is tender, use forks or tongs to shred it directly in the pot.
   - Add the chopped carrots and potatoes to the pot and continue to simmer until the vegetables are cooked through and tender.
5. **Serve:**
   - Remove the bay leaves and whole cloves.
   - Serve the Hilachas hot, garnished with chopped fresh cilantro if desired, alongside cooked rice and warm corn tortillas.

Hilachas is a comforting and flavorful dish that's often served as a main course for lunch or dinner. Its rich tomato-based sauce and tender beef make it a beloved meal in Guatemala. Adjust the seasoning and spice levels according to your preference. Enjoy your homemade Guatemalan Hilachas!

Revolcado

Serves: 6-8 Prep time: 20 min Cook time: 3 hrs

INGREDIENTS

2 pounds pork shoulder or pork belly, cut into chunks

1 onion, chopped

4-5 tomatoes, chopped

4-5 cloves garlic, minced

2 bell peppers (1 red, 1 green), chopped

2 carrots, peeled and chopped

2-3 potatoes, peeled and diced

4-5 guaque chilies (or substitute with mild dried chili peppers)

4-5 whole cloves

2 bay leaves

1 teaspoon dried oregano

1 teaspoon ground cumin

1 teaspoon paprika

1 teaspoon achiote powder or paste (optional, for color)

Salt and pepper to taste
Vegetable oil for cooking
Chopped fresh cilantro for garnish (optional)
Cooked rice or tortillas for serving

DIRECTIONS

1. **Prepare the Pork:**
   - In a large pot or Dutch oven, heat some vegetable oil over medium-high heat.
   - Add the pork chunks and brown them on all sides for a few minutes.
2. **Create the Base:**
   - Once the pork is browned, add the chopped onion and minced garlic. Sauté until they become translucent and fragrant.
   - Add the chopped tomatoes and bell peppers. Cook until the tomatoes break down and form a thick sauce.
3. **Spice It Up:**
   - Add the guaque chilies (or dried chili peppers), whole cloves, bay leaves, dried oregano, ground cumin, paprika, achiote powder (if using), salt, and pepper to the pot. Stir well.
4. **Cook the Stew:**
   - Add enough water to cover the pork and spices. Stir to combine.
   - Bring the mixture to a boil, then reduce the heat to low, cover the pot, and let it simmer for about 2-3 hours until the pork is tender and the flavors have melded together.
5. **Add Vegetables and Serve:**
   - Once the pork is tender, add the chopped carrots and potatoes to the pot. Simmer until the vegetables are cooked through but not mushy.
   - Remove the bay leaves and whole cloves.
   - Serve the Revolcado hot, garnished with chopped fresh cilantro if desired. It's commonly served with rice or warm tortillas.

Revolcado is a delicious and aromatic dish with a rich blend of spices and tender pork that's enjoyed in Guatemala. Adjust the spiciness by modifying the amount of chili peppers used. Enjoy your homemade Guatemalan Revolcado!

Jocon

Serves: 6-8   Prep time: 20 min   Cook time: 2 hrs

INGREDIENTS

3-4 pounds chicken pieces (such as thighs and drumsticks)

1 onion, chopped

4-5 tomatillos, husks removed and chopped

4-5 cloves garlic, minced

2 bell peppers (1 green, 1 red), chopped

2-3 jalapeño or serrano peppers (adjust for desired spiciness), chopped

1 bunch fresh cilantro, stems and leaves separated

1 bunch fresh mint leaves

2-3 tablespoons pumpkin seeds (pepitas)

2-3 tablespoons sesame seeds

4-5 whole cloves

1 teaspoon ground cumin

1 teaspoon dried oregano

4 cups chicken broth

Vegetable oil for cooking

Salt and pepper to taste

Cooked rice or corn tortillas for serving

DIRECTIONS

1. **Brown the Chicken:**
   - In a large pot or Dutch oven, heat some vegetable oil over medium-high heat.
   - Add the chicken pieces and brown them on all sides. Remove them from the pot and set aside.
2. **Create the Green Sauce:**
   - In the same pot, add a bit more oil if needed. Sauté the chopped onion, minced garlic, tomatillos, chopped bell peppers, and jalapeño or serrano peppers until they begin to soften.
   - In a blender or food processor, combine the sautéed mixture with cilantro stems, mint leaves, pumpkin seeds, sesame seeds, whole cloves, ground cumin, dried oregano, salt, pepper, and 2 cups of chicken broth. Blend until you get a smooth green sauce.
3. **Cook the Chicken in the Green Sauce:**
   - Return the browned chicken pieces to the pot and pour the green sauce over them.
   - Add the remaining 2 cups of chicken broth to the pot. Stir well to combine.
   - Bring the mixture to a boil, then reduce the heat to low, cover the pot, and let it simmer for about 1.5 to 2 hours until the chicken is cooked through and tender.
4. **Serve:**
   - Once ready, taste the Jocon and adjust seasoning if necessary.
   - Serve the Jocon hot over cooked rice or with warm corn tortillas.

Jocon is a vibrant and aromatic dish that beautifully showcases the flavors of Guatemala. The green sauce, enriched with tomatillos, herbs, and spices, infuses the chicken with a delightful taste. Enjoy your homemade Guatemalan Jocon!

Shucos

Serves: 4 Prep time: 20 min Cook time: 15 min

INGREDIENTS

4 large hot dog sausages (frankfurters or sausages of your choice)

4 hot dog buns

1 cup shredded cabbage

1 cup chopped cooked or pickled beets

1 cup guacamole (prepared or homemade)

1 cup cooked or fried onions

1 cup cooked bacon bits or crumbled chorizo (optional)

1 cup mayonnaise or crema (sour cream)

1 cup ketchup

1 cup mustard

1 cup finely chopped tomatoes

1 cup chopped green onions or chives

1 cup hot sauce or salsa picante (optional)

Vegetable oil for cooking

DIRECTIONS

1. **Prepare the Toppings:**
   - Cook the bacon bits or chorizo if using and set aside.
   - Chop and prepare all the other toppings: shredded cabbage, chopped beets, guacamole, cooked onions, chopped tomatoes, green onions or chives.
2. **Cook the Sausages:**
   - In a skillet or on a grill, cook the hot dog sausages until they are browned and cooked through. Remove and set aside.
3. **Prepare the Buns:**
   - Lightly toast the hot dog buns on the skillet or grill, if desired.
4. **Assemble the Shucos:**
   - Take each hot dog bun and place a cooked sausage inside.
   - Layer the toppings: Start with shredded cabbage, followed by chopped beets, guacamole, cooked onions, bacon bits or crumbled chorizo (if using), chopped tomatoes, green onions or chives.
   - Drizzle with mayonnaise or crema, ketchup, mustard, and hot sauce or salsa picante if desired.
5. **Serve:**
   - Serve the Shucos immediately while they're still warm and loaded with toppings.

Shucos are known for their generous toppings and can be customized to your taste. You can add or omit toppings based on your preferences. Enjoy your homemade Guatemalan Shucos!

Fiambre

Serves: Varies Prep time: Varies Cook time: Varies

INGREDIENTS

Fiambre consists of a variety of meats, vegetables, and pickled items. This recipe includes many ingredients, and the quantities can be adjusted based on personal preferences. The following list includes common ingredients used in Fiambre:

Cold cuts: sliced ham, turkey, sausages, and other deli meats

Cooked chicken, beef, or pork, shredded or diced

Assorted vegetables: carrots, green beans, peas, beets, cauliflower, broccoli, asparagus, and bell peppers (all blanched or pickled)

Cheese: diced or cubed (queso seco or other hard cheeses)

Hard-boiled eggs, sliced or halved

Olives: green and black

Pickled vegetables: jalapeños, onions, radishes, and baby corn

Condiments: capers, pickles, and pickled peppers

Lettuce leaves for lining the serving dish

DIRECTIONS

1. Prepare the Ingredients:

- Cook and prepare all the meats, allowing them to cool before assembling.
- Cut, dice, or slice the vegetables, cheeses, and hard-boiled eggs.
- If making pickled vegetables, prepare these ahead of time. Blanching vegetables can also be done in advance.

2. Assemble the Fiambre:

- Fiambre is traditionally arranged on a large serving platter or in individual bowls.
- Begin by lining the serving dish with lettuce leaves.
- Arrange the various ingredients in sections or rows, allowing each component to have its own space on the platter. There's no fixed order; it's about creating an aesthetically pleasing display of colors and textures.

3. Serve:

- Fiambre is typically served cold. It's recommended to refrigerate it for a few hours or overnight to allow the flavors to meld together.

Fiambre is a dish meant to be shared with family and friends. The preparation can be a communal activity, with each family member contributing to the dish. The variety of ingredients reflects the cultural diversity and the blending of flavors in Guatemalan cuisine. Adjust the ingredients and proportions to suit your taste preferences. Enjoy this unique and festive dish!

Rellenitos

Serves: 4-6 Prep time: 20 min Cook time: 30 min

INGREDIENTS

For the Mashed Plantains:

4 ripe plantains

1/4 cup of sugar

1/2 teaspoon of ground cinnamon

A pinch of salt

Vegetable oil for frying

For the Sweet Bean Filling:

1 cup of cooked black beans (canned or cooked from dried)

1/4 cup of sugar

1/2 teaspoon of ground cinnamon

1/4 teaspoon of ground cloves

A pinch of salt

DIRECTIONS

1. **Prepare the Sweet Bean Filling:**
   - In a saucepan, combine the cooked black beans, sugar, ground cinnamon, ground cloves, and a pinch of salt.
   - Cook the mixture over low heat, stirring constantly, until it thickens and resembles a sweet bean paste. This should take about 10-15 minutes.
   - Once done, remove it from heat and let it cool.
2. **Prepare the Mashed Plantains:**
   - Peel the ripe plantains and cut them into chunks.
   - In a pot of boiling water, cook the plantain chunks until they are soft and can be easily mashed with a fork.
   - Drain the plantains and place them in a mixing bowl.
3. **Mash and Season the Plantains:**
   - Mash the cooked plantains until smooth.
   - Add sugar, ground cinnamon, and a pinch of salt to the mashed plantains. Mix well to combine the seasonings.
4. **Form the Rellenitos:**
   - Take a portion of the mashed plantains and flatten it in the palm of your hand to form a small circle.
   - Place a spoonful of the sweet bean filling in the center of the plantain circle.
   - Carefully enclose the sweet bean filling within the mashed plantains, shaping it into a ball or oval shape.
   - Repeat this process for the remaining plantains and sweet bean filling.
5. **Fry the Rellenitos:**
   - In a large skillet or frying pan, heat vegetable oil over medium-high heat.
   - Carefully place the rellenitos in the hot oil and fry them until they are golden brown and crispy on the outside. This should take about 3-5 minutes per side.
   - Remove the fried rellenitos and place them on paper towels to drain excess oil.

6. Serve:

- Serve Guatemalan Rellenitos hot as a delightful dessert or snack.

Guatemalan Rellenitos are a popular and traditional sweet treat that combines the natural sweetness of ripe plantains with a luscious sweet bean filling. They're often enjoyed as a delicious snack or dessert in Guatemalan cuisine. Enjoy!

Arroz en Leche

Serves: 4-6 Prep time: 15 min Cook time: 1 hr

INGREDIENTS

1 cup of long-grain white rice

4 cups of whole milk

1 cup of water

1 cinnamon stick

1/2 cup of sugar (adjust to taste)

1/2 cup of raisins

1/4 teaspoon of ground cinnamon

1/4 teaspoon of ground nutmeg

1/4 teaspoon of salt

1 teaspoon of vanilla extract

Grated zest of 1 lemon (optional)

Grated zest of 1 orange (optional)

Cinnamon sticks and extra ground cinnamon for garnish

DIRECTIONS

1. **Rinse and Prepare the Rice:**
   - Rinse the white rice under cold water until the water runs clear.
   - Drain the rice and set it aside.
2. **Cook the Rice:**
   - In a large pot, combine the rinsed rice, milk, water, and cinnamon stick.
   - Bring the mixture to a boil over medium-high heat, stirring occasionally.
   - Once it starts to boil, reduce the heat to low and simmer, uncovered, for about 30-40 minutes, or until the rice is soft and the mixture has thickened.
   - Stir occasionally to prevent the rice from sticking to the bottom of the pot.
3. **Add Sugar and Flavorings:**
   - Stir in the sugar, ground cinnamon, ground nutmeg, salt, raisins, vanilla extract, and optional lemon and orange zest.
   - Continue to simmer for another 5-10 minutes, or until the rice pudding is creamy and well flavored.
4. **Remove the Cinnamon Stick:**
   - Remove the cinnamon stick from the pot and discard it.
5. **Serve:**
   - Serve Guatemalan Arroz en Leche warm or at room temperature.
   - Garnish with extra ground cinnamon and a cinnamon stick if desired.

Guatemalan Arroz en Leche is a creamy and comforting rice pudding that's flavored with aromatic spices and a hint of citrus. It's a delightful dessert that is enjoyed in Guatemala and throughout Latin America. Enjoy!

Champurradas

Serves: 12pcs Prep time: 20 min Cook time: 25 min

INGREDIENTS

2 cups of all-purpose flour

1 cup of granulated sugar

1/2 cup of vegetable oil or melted butter

1/4 cup of milk

1 teaspoon of baking powder

1/2 teaspoon of ground cinnamon

1/4 teaspoon of salt

1/4 cup of sesame seeds

1/4 cup of finely chopped nuts (walnuts or pecans)

1 teaspoon of vanilla extract

DIRECTIONS

1. **Preheat the Oven:**
   - Preheat your oven to 350°F (175°C). Line a baking sheet with parchment paper or lightly grease it.
2. **Mix Dry Ingredients:**
   - In a mixing bowl, combine the all-purpose flour, granulated sugar, baking powder, ground cinnamon, salt, sesame seeds, and chopped nuts.
3. **Add Wet Ingredients:**
   - Add the vegetable oil (or melted butter), milk, and vanilla extract to the dry ingredients.
   - Mix well to form a cohesive dough.
4. **Shape the Champurradas:**
   - Take a small portion of the dough and roll it into a ball about the size of a walnut.
   - Place the ball on the prepared baking sheet.
5. **Flatten and Decorate:**
   - Use a flat-bottomed glass or a cookie stamp to gently flatten each dough ball into a round cookie shape.
   - You can also use a fork to make a crisscross pattern on top for decoration.
6. **Bake:**
   - Place the baking sheet with the champurradas in the preheated oven.
   - Bake for about 20-25 minutes or until they turn golden brown around the edges.
7. **Cool and Serve:**
   - Remove the champurradas from the oven and let them cool on a wire rack.
   - Once they have cooled completely, they are ready to serve.

Guatemalan Champurradas are delicious cookies with a crunchy texture and a sweet, nutty flavor. They are a popular snack or dessert in Guatemalan cuisine and are perfect for enjoying with a cup of coffee or tea. Enjoy your homemade champurradas!

Tapado

Serves: 4-6 Prep time: 20 min Cook time: 40 min

INGREDIENTS

For the Broth:

4 cups of coconut milk

4 cups of fish or seafood broth (you can make your own or use store-bought)

2 tablespoons of vegetable oil

1 onion, finely chopped

4 cloves of garlic, minced

1 red bell pepper, finely chopped

1 green bell pepper, finely chopped

2 tomatoes, diced

1/2 teaspoon of ground cumin

1/2 teaspoon of ground achiote (annatto) for color (optional)

Salt and black pepper, to taste

For the Seafood:

1 pound of firm white fish fillets, cut into chunks

1/2 pound of large shrimp, peeled and deveined

1/2 pound of mussels, cleaned and debearded

1/2 pound of small clams, cleaned

1/2 pound of squid rings and tentacles

1/2 cup of fresh cilantro leaves

1/4 cup of chopped fresh parsley

Lime wedges, for serving

Sliced red onion and jalapeño rings, for garnish (optional)

DIRECTIONS

1. **Prepare the Broth:**
   - In a large pot, heat the vegetable oil over medium-high heat.
   - Add the finely chopped onion and cook until it becomes translucent.
   - Stir in the minced garlic, chopped red and green bell peppers, and diced tomatoes.
   - Cook for about 5-7 minutes, or until the vegetables are soft and fragrant.
   - Add the ground cumin and ground achiote for color (if using). Stir to combine.
   - Pour in the coconut milk and fish or seafood broth, and season with salt and black pepper.
   - Bring the broth to a gentle simmer and let it cook for about 10-15 minutes, allowing the flavors to meld.
2. **Add the Seafood:**
   - Once the broth has simmered and developed flavor, add the fish fillets, shrimp, mussels, clams, and squid rings and tentacles.
   - Simmer for an additional 5-7 minutes, or until the seafood is cooked through. The mussels and clams should open when they are done.

3. Serve:

- Serve Guatemalan Tapado hot, garnished with fresh cilantro and parsley.
- Offer lime wedges, and if desired, garnish with sliced red onion and jalapeño rings for extra heat and flavor.

Guatemalan Tapado is a delightful and rich seafood stew that combines the fresh flavors of various seafood ingredients with the creaminess of coconut milk and aromatic spices. It's a popular dish in Guatemalan coastal regions and is perfect for seafood lovers. Enjoy!

Section 5

Honduras

Baleadas

Serves: 4-6   Prep time: 20 min   Cook time: 15 min

INGREDIENTS

For the Flour Tortillas:

2 cups of all-purpose flour

1 teaspoon of baking powder

1/2 teaspoon of salt

2 tablespoons of vegetable oil

3/4 cup of warm water

For the Filling:

2 cups of refried black beans (you can use canned refried beans or make your own)

1 cup of crumbled queso fresco (fresh cheese) or queso duro (hard cheese)

1 cup of sour cream or crema (you can use Honduran-style crema if available)

2 ripe avocados, sliced

1 cup of diced cooked meat (such as grilled beef, chicken, or chorizo)

Salsa or hot sauce, for serving (optional)

DIRECTIONS

1. **Prepare the Flour Tortillas:**
    - In a mixing bowl, combine the all-purpose flour, baking powder, and salt.
    - Add the vegetable oil and warm water to the dry ingredients.
    - Knead the mixture until it forms a smooth, elastic dough. If the dough is too sticky, add a bit more flour.
    - Divide the dough into small balls, about the size of a golf ball.
    - Roll each ball into a thin, round tortilla using a rolling pin or your hands.
2. **Cook the Tortillas:**
    - Heat a dry skillet or griddle over medium-high heat.
    - Cook the tortillas one at a time, flipping them when they begin to puff up and have light brown spots. Each tortilla should take about 1-2 minutes per side.
    - Place the cooked tortillas on a plate and cover with a clean kitchen towel to keep them warm and soft.
3. **Assemble the Baleadas:**
    - Spread a generous portion of refried black beans on each tortilla.
    - Sprinkle crumbled queso fresco or queso duro over the beans.
    - Add sliced avocados and diced cooked meat to each tortilla.
    - Top with a dollop of sour cream or crema.
    - Optionally, add salsa or hot sauce for extra flavor.
4. **Serve:**
    - Fold each tortilla in half to encase the fillings and serve Honduran Baleadas hot.

Honduran Baleadas are a beloved street food in Honduras, featuring soft flour tortillas filled with a variety of delicious ingredients. They are a popular and satisfying meal that can be customized to your taste. Enjoy!

Carne Asada

Serves: 4-6 Prep time: 15 min Cook time: 15 min

INGREDIENTS

2 pounds flank steak or skirt steak

½ cup orange juice

¼ cup lime juice

4 cloves garlic, minced

1 onion, finely chopped

½ cup fresh cilantro, chopped

2 teaspoons ground cumin

2 teaspoons paprika

1 teaspoon dried oregano

Salt and pepper to taste

2 tablespoons vegetable oil (for grilling)

Sliced limes and fresh cilantro for garnish (optional)

DIRECTIONS

1. **Prepare the Marinade:**
   - In a mixing bowl, combine the orange juice, lime juice, minced garlic, chopped onion, chopped cilantro, ground cumin, paprika, dried oregano, salt, and pepper. Mix well to form the marinade.
2. **Marinate the Steak:**
   - Place the flank steak or skirt steak in a shallow dish or a resealable plastic bag.
   - Pour the marinade over the meat, ensuring it's well coated. Cover the dish or seal the bag and refrigerate for at least 2-4 hours, allowing the flavors to infuse into the meat.
3. **Preheat the Grill:**
   - Preheat your grill to medium-high heat. Brush the grill grates lightly with vegetable oil to prevent sticking.
4. **Grill the Steak:**
   - Remove the marinated steak from the refrigerator and let it sit at room temperature for about 15-20 minutes before grilling.
   - Place the steak on the preheated grill and cook for approximately 5-7 minutes on each side, or until desired doneness is reached. The cooking time may vary based on the thickness of the steak and your preferred level of doneness (medium-rare, medium, etc.).
5. **Rest and Serve:**
   - Once cooked to your liking, remove the steak from the grill and let it rest for 5 minutes before slicing.
   - Slice the carne asada against the grain into thin strips.
   - Garnish with sliced limes and fresh cilantro if desired.
   - Serve the Honduran Carne Asada with sides like rice, beans, tortillas, or a fresh salad.

Honduran Carne Asada is a mouthwatering dish that showcases the vibrant flavors of Central America. Adjust the marinade ingredients to suit your taste preferences. Enjoy your homemade Honduran Carne Asada!

Pastelitos de Perro

Serves: 9pcs Prep time: 30 min Cook time: 30 min

INGREDIENTS

For the Dough:

4 cups all-purpose flour

1 cup warm water

1 teaspoon salt

½ cup vegetable shortening or lard

1 teaspoon baking powder

For the Filling:

1 pound ground beef

1 onion, finely chopped

2 cloves garlic, minced

1 bell pepper, finely chopped

1 teaspoon ground cumin

1 teaspoon paprika

Salt and pepper to taste

Vegetable oil for frying

DIRECTIONS

1. **Make the Dough:**
   - In a large mixing bowl, combine the flour, salt, and baking powder. Add the vegetable shortening or lard and mix until the mixture resembles coarse crumbs.
   - Slowly add the warm water and knead until a smooth dough forms. Cover the dough with a clean kitchen towel and let it rest for about 15-20 minutes.
2. **Prepare the Filling:**
   - In a skillet, heat a little vegetable oil over medium heat. Add the chopped onion, garlic, and bell pepper. Sauté until they soften.
   - Add the ground beef to the skillet and cook until it's browned and cooked through.
   - Season the beef mixture with ground cumin, paprika, salt, and pepper. Mix well and let it simmer for a few minutes. Remove from heat and let it cool.
3. **Assemble the Pastelitos:**
   - Divide the rested dough into small balls, about the size of a golf ball. Roll out each ball into a thin circle (about 4-5 inches in diameter) on a floured surface.
   - Place a spoonful of the cooled beef filling onto one half of the dough circle, leaving space around the edges.
   - Fold the other half of the dough over the filling to create a half-moon shape. Press the edges together firmly, then use a fork to seal the edges.
4. **Fry the Pastelitos:**
   - In a deep skillet or frying pan, heat vegetable oil over medium-high heat.
   - Carefully place the assembled pastelitos into the hot oil and fry until they turn golden brown on both sides, flipping once to ensure even cooking.
   - Once cooked, remove the pastelitos from the oil and place them on a paper towel-lined plate to drain excess oil.
5. **Serve:**
   - Serve the Honduran Pastelitos de Perro hot and crispy. They can be enjoyed on their own or with a side of salsa, hot sauce, or a tangy coleslaw.

These pastelitos are delicious as a snack or a meal and are perfect for sharing with family and friends! Adjust the seasoning of the filling according to your taste preferences.

Tamales

Serves: 12pcs Prep time: 1.5 hrs Cook time: 2.5 hrs

INGREDIENTS

For the Dough (Masa):

3 cups of masa harina (corn dough)

1/2 cup of vegetable oil

3 cups of chicken or vegetable broth

1 teaspoon of salt

1/2 teaspoon of achiote (annatto) paste (optional, for color)

For the Filling:

2 cups of cooked and shredded chicken (you can also use pork or beef)

1 cup of cooked and diced vegetables (carrots, bell peppers, green beans, peas)

1/2 cup of tomato sauce

1/2 cup of green olives, pitted and sliced

1/2 cup of raisins

1/4 cup of capers

1/4 cup of diced bell peppers

1/4 cup of diced onions

2 cloves of garlic, minced

1 teaspoon of ground cumin

Salt and black pepper, to taste

For Assembling and Wrapping:

Banana leaves or aluminum foil, cut into squares

Kitchen twine or strips of banana leaves for tying

DIRECTIONS

1. **Prepare the Filling:**
   - In a large skillet, heat a bit of vegetable oil over medium-high heat.
   - Add the diced onions, bell peppers, and garlic. Sauté until they become soft and translucent.
   - Add the cooked and shredded chicken, diced vegetables, tomato sauce, green olives, raisins, capers, ground cumin, salt, and black pepper.
   - Cook for about 5-7 minutes, or until the filling is well combined and slightly thickened. Remove from heat and set it aside.
2. **Prepare the Masa (Dough):**
   - In a large mixing bowl, combine the masa harina, vegetable oil, chicken or vegetable broth, salt, and achiote paste (if using).
   - Knead the mixture until it forms a soft, pliable dough. If the dough is too dry, you can add a little more broth to achieve the right consistency.
3. **Assemble the Tamales:**
   - Lay out a banana leaf or aluminum foil square on a clean work surface.
   - Place a portion of masa dough in the center of the leaf or foil and press it into a rectangle shape.
   - Spoon a portion of the prepared filling on top of the masa.

- Carefully fold the banana leaf or foil over the filling, creating a rectangle package.
- Secure the tamales with kitchen twine or strips of banana leaves.

4. **Steam the Tamales:**

- In a large steamer, arrange the tamales vertically, standing on their folded ends.
- Steam the tamales for about 2-2.5 hours, or until they become firm and fully cooked.
- Check the water level in the steamer periodically and add more boiling water as needed.

5. **Serve:**

- Remove the tamales from the steamer and let them cool slightly before unwrapping.
- Serve Honduran Tamales hot and enjoy this traditional Central American delicacy.

Honduran Tamales are a labor of love, and they are often prepared for special occasions and holidays. The combination of the tender masa and flavorful filling is sure to be a hit.

Tajadas

Serves: 4-6   Prep time: 10 min   Cook time: 20 min

INGREDIENTS

4 ripe plantains, peeled and sliced diagonally into 1/2-inch thick pieces

Vegetable oil for frying

Salt, to taste

Crumbled queso duro or queso fresco (hard or fresh cheese) for garnish (optional)

DIRECTIONS

1. **Heat the Oil:**
   - In a deep skillet or frying pan, heat enough vegetable oil over medium-high heat to submerge the plantain slices.
2. **Fry the Plantains:**
   - Carefully add the plantain slices to the hot oil.
   - Fry the plantains in batches, making sure not to overcrowd the pan. You want them to have enough space to cook evenly.

- Fry the plantains for about 2-3 minutes per side, or until they turn golden brown and crispy.
- Use a slotted spoon to remove the fried plantains and place them on paper towels to drain excess oil.

3. **Flatten and Season:**
   - Once the plantains are drained, use a tostonera (plantain press) or the bottom of a heavy glass to flatten each slice to about 1/4 inch thick.
   - Return the flattened plantains to the hot oil and fry for an additional 1-2 minutes on each side until they are crispy and lightly golden.
4. **Season and Serve:**
   - Remove the tajadas from the oil and place them on paper towels to remove excess oil.
   - Sprinkle the fried plantains with salt to taste.
   - Optionally, garnish with crumbled queso duro or queso fresco for added flavor.
5. Serve:
   - Serve Honduran Tajadas hot as a delicious side dish or snack. They are often served with a side of refried beans and sour cream.

Honduran Tajadas are a beloved and classic Honduran dish made from fried ripe plantains. They are sweet, savory, and delightfully crispy. Enjoy this popular Central American treat!

Arroz con Pollo

Serves: 4-6 Prep time: 20 min Cook time: 50 min

INGREDIENTS

For the Chicken and Marinade:

2 pounds of chicken pieces (such as thighs and drumsticks)

2 cloves of garlic, minced

1 teaspoon of ground cumin

1 teaspoon of dried oregano

Salt and black pepper, to taste

Juice of 1 lime

For the Rice:

2 cups of long-grain white rice

3 cups of chicken broth

1 tablespoon of vegetable oil

1 onion, finely chopped

1 bell pepper (red or green), finely chopped

2 cloves of garlic, minced

1/2 cup of frozen peas

1/2 cup of diced carrots

1/2 cup of diced green beans

1/4 cup of tomato sauce

Salt and black pepper, to taste

Saffron threads or a pinch of ground turmeric (for color, optional)

DIRECTIONS

1. **Marinate the Chicken:**
   - In a large bowl, combine the minced garlic, ground cumin, dried oregano, salt, black pepper, and lime juice.
   - Add the chicken pieces to the marinade and coat them well.
   - Cover and let the chicken marinate for at least 30 minutes, or refrigerate for a few hours for better flavor.
2. **Cook the Chicken:**
   - In a large skillet or Dutch oven, heat vegetable oil over medium-high heat.
   - Add the marinated chicken pieces and cook until they are browned on all sides.
   - Remove the chicken from the pan and set it aside.
3. **Sauté the Aromatics:**
   - In the same pan, add chopped onions and bell peppers. Sauté until they become soft and translucent.
   - Add minced garlic and sauté for an additional minute.
4. **Cook the Rice:**
   - Add the white rice to the pan and stir to combine with the aromatics.
   - Pour in the chicken broth and tomato sauce. Stir well.
   - Add frozen peas, diced carrots, and green beans.

- Season with salt and black pepper, and add saffron threads or a pinch of ground turmeric for color (if desired).
- Return the cooked chicken to the pan.

5. **Simmer and Cook:**
   - Reduce the heat to low, cover the pan, and let the mixture simmer for about 25-30 minutes, or until the rice is cooked and the chicken is tender.

6. **Serve:**
   - Serve Honduran Arroz con Pollo hot, garnished with fresh cilantro or parsley if desired.

Honduran Arroz con Pollo is a hearty and flavorful dish that combines tender chicken and aromatic rice, making it a popular choice for family dinners and gatherings. Enjoy!

Yuca con Chicharron

Serves: 4-6 Prep time: 30 min Cook time: 1 hr

INGREDIENTS

For the Chicharrón (Fried Pork):

1 pound of pork belly or pork rinds, cut into small pieces

Vegetable oil for frying

Salt and black pepper, to taste

For the Yuca (Cassava):

2 pounds of fresh cassava (yuca)

Water for boiling

Salt, to taste

For the Curtido (Pickled Cabbage Slaw):

2 cups of shredded cabbage

1/2 cup of diced white onion

1/2 cup of white vinegar

1/4 cup of water

1 teaspoon of dried oregano

Salt and black pepper, to taste

Hot sauce (optional)

DIRECTIONS

1. **Prepare the Chicharrón (Fried Pork):**
   - In a large skillet or deep fryer, heat vegetable oil over medium-high heat.
   - Add the pork pieces and fry them until they are crispy and golden brown. This may take about 15-20 minutes.
   - Remove the fried pork from the oil and place it on paper towels to drain excess oil.
   - Season with salt and black pepper to taste.
2. **Prepare the Yuca (Cassava):**
   - Peel the cassava and cut it into 3-inch-long pieces.
   - In a large pot, bring water to a boil.
   - Add the cassava pieces and cook for about 20-30 minutes, or until they are tender and easily pierced with a fork.
   - Drain the cooked cassava and season with salt.
3. **Prepare the Curtido (Pickled Cabbage Slaw):**
   - In a bowl, combine the shredded cabbage and diced white onion.
   - In a separate bowl, mix the white vinegar, water, dried oregano, salt, black pepper, and hot sauce (if using).
   - Pour the vinegar mixture over the cabbage and onion.
   - Toss the ingredients to combine and let the curtido sit for at least 30 minutes to marinate.
4. **Serve:**
   - Serve Honduran Yuca con Chicharrón with the fried pork on top of the cassava.
   - Serve the curtido on the side as a refreshing, tangy accompaniment.

Honduran Yuca con Chicharrón is a delicious and satisfying dish that combines the earthy flavors of cassava with the crispy goodness of fried pork. The curtido adds a zesty and tangy contrast to the meal. Enjoy!

Macheteadas

Serves: 7pcs Prep time: 15 min Cook time: 15 min

INGREDIENTS

4 cups of all-purpose flour

1 cup of sugar

1/2 cup of vegetable oil

1/4 cup of butter, softened

2 eggs

1/2 cup of milk

1 teaspoon of baking powder

1/2 teaspoon of ground cinnamon

1/4 teaspoon of salt

Zest of 1 orange (optional)

Zest of 1 lemon (optional)

Vegetable oil for frying

Powdered sugar, for dusting (optional)

DIRECTIONS

1. **Prepare the Dough:**
   - In a large mixing bowl, combine the all-purpose flour, sugar, baking powder, ground cinnamon, and salt.
   - Add the softened butter and vegetable oil. Mix until the mixture resembles coarse crumbs.
2. **Add Wet Ingredients:**
   - Beat the eggs and add them to the mixture.
   - Add the milk and citrus zest (if using).
   - Stir the ingredients until they form a smooth and elastic dough. You can adjust the consistency by adding more flour or milk if needed.
3. **Roll and Cut the Dough:**
   - On a lightly floured surface, roll out the dough into a large rectangle, about 1/4 inch thick.
4. **Fry the Macheteadas:**
   - Heat vegetable oil in a deep skillet or frying pan over medium-high heat.
   - Carefully cut the rolled dough into rectangles or squares, about 3-4 inches in size.
   - Fry the macheteadas in the hot oil until they are puffed and golden brown, about 2-3 minutes per side.
   - Remove them from the oil and place them on paper towels to drain excess oil.
5. **Serve:**
   - Serve Honduran Macheteadas hot and, if desired, dusted with powdered sugar for added sweetness.

Honduran Macheteadas are a delightful sweet treat with a crispy texture and a hint of cinnamon and citrus. They are often enjoyed as a snack or dessert and are a popular part of Honduran cuisine. Enjoy!

Sopa de Caracol

Serves: 6-8   Prep time: 20 min   Cook time: 1 hr

INGREDIENTS

For the Soup:

2 pounds of conch meat, cleaned and cut into small pieces

1 onion, finely chopped

2 cloves of garlic, minced

1 red bell pepper, finely chopped

1 green bell pepper, finely chopped

2 tomatoes, diced

2 carrots, peeled and sliced

2 potatoes, peeled and diced

4 cups of fish or seafood broth (you can make your own or use store-bought)

1 cup of coconut milk

2 cups of water

2-3 sprigs of thyme

2-3 sprigs of fresh cilantro

2-3 sprigs of fresh parsley

1/2 teaspoon of ground cumin

1/2 teaspoon of ground achiote (annatto) for color (optional)

2 tablespoons of vegetable oil

Salt and black pepper, to taste

For Garnish:

Lime wedges

Sliced red onion and jalapeño rings

Fresh cilantro leaves

DIRECTIONS

1. **Prepare the Conch:**
   - If using fresh conch, clean and rinse it thoroughly. You can tenderize it by pounding it with a mallet or rolling pin.
   - Cut the conch meat into small pieces.
2. **Sauté the Aromatics:**
   - In a large pot, heat the vegetable oil over medium-high heat.
   - Add the finely chopped onion and cook until it becomes translucent.
   - Stir in the minced garlic, chopped red and green bell peppers, and diced tomatoes.
   - Cook for about 5-7 minutes, or until the vegetables are soft and fragrant.
3. **Cook the Soup:**
   - Add the conch pieces to the pot and cook for a few minutes until they turn white.
   - Pour in the fish or seafood broth, coconut milk, and water.
   - Add the sliced carrots and diced potatoes.
   - Season with ground cumin, ground achiote (if using), salt, and black pepper.
   - Tie the sprigs of thyme, cilantro, and parsley together with kitchen twine and add them to the pot.

- Let the soup simmer for about 30-40 minutes, or until the conch is tender and the vegetables are cooked.

4. **Serve:**

- Serve Honduran Sopa de Caracol hot, garnished with lime wedges, sliced red onion and jalapeño rings, and fresh cilantro leaves.

Honduran Sopa de Caracol is a flavorful and hearty seafood soup featuring tender conch, vegetables, and aromatic herbs. It's a beloved dish along the Honduran coast and is perfect for seafood enthusiasts. Enjoy!

Section 6

Nicaragua

Gallo Pinto

Serves: 4-6 Prep time: 15 min Cook time: 20 min

INGREDIENTS

2 cups of cooked white rice

2 cups of cooked red beans (or black beans), with some liquid

2 tablespoons of vegetable oil

1 small onion, finely chopped

1 red bell pepper, finely chopped

2 cloves of garlic, minced

1/2 cup of cooked and crumbled chorizo (optional)

1/2 teaspoon of ground cumin

1/2 teaspoon of ground achiote (annatto) for color (optional)

Salt and black pepper, to taste

Chopped fresh cilantro, for garnish

Sliced green onions, for garnish

DIRECTIONS

1. **Sauté the Aromatics:**
   - In a large skillet, heat the vegetable oil over medium-high heat.
   - Add the finely chopped onion and cook until it becomes translucent.
   - Stir in the minced garlic and chopped red bell pepper. Sauté until they are soft and fragrant.
2. **Add the Beans:**
   - Add the cooked beans with some of their cooking liquid to the skillet.
   - Stir in the ground cumin and ground achiote (if using) for color.
   - Cook for a few minutes, allowing the flavors to meld.
3. **Combine with Rice:**
   - Add the cooked white rice to the skillet and mix it with the bean mixture.
   - Stir well to combine all the ingredients evenly.
   - If using cooked and crumbled chorizo, add it at this stage and mix.
4. **Season:**
   - Season the Gallo Pinto with salt and black pepper to taste. Adjust the seasoning as needed.
5. **Serve:**
   - Serve Nicaraguan Gallo Pinto hot, garnished with chopped fresh cilantro and sliced green onions.

Nicaraguan Gallo Pinto is a classic and delicious rice and beans dish that's often enjoyed for breakfast or as a side dish in Nicaragua. It's easy to prepare and is loved for its savory and comforting flavors. Enjoy!

Desayuno Nica

Serves: 4 Prep time: 15 min Cook time: 25 min

INGREDIENTS

2 cups cooked rice

2 cups cooked red or black beans

2 tablespoons vegetable oil

1 small onion, finely chopped

2 cloves garlic, minced

1 red bell pepper, diced

1 teaspoon ground cumin

Salt and pepper to taste

4 eggs

2 ripe plantains

Nicaraguan cheese or any white cheese (queso fresco), sliced or crumbled

Crema (sour cream) for serving (optional)

Chopped cilantro or green onions for garnish (optional)

DIRECTIONS

1. **Prepare Gallo Pinto:**
   - In a skillet or frying pan, heat the vegetable oil over medium heat. Add the chopped onion, minced garlic, and diced red bell pepper. Sauté until the vegetables are soft and translucent.
   - Add the cooked rice and cooked beans to the skillet. Stir well to combine. Sprinkle with ground cumin, salt, and pepper. Cook for 5-7 minutes, stirring occasionally until heated through. Set aside and keep warm.
2. **Cook the Eggs:**
   - In another skillet, heat a little oil over medium heat. Crack the eggs into the skillet and cook them according to your preference (fried, scrambled, or sunny-side-up). Season with salt and pepper.
3. **Fry the Plantains:**
   - Peel the ripe plantains and cut them into thick slices. In the same skillet used for the eggs, fry the plantain slices until golden brown on each side, about 2-3 minutes per side.
4. **Assemble the Breakfast:**
   - Divide the Gallo Pinto among serving plates.
   - Arrange the cooked eggs and fried plantains on the plates alongside the Gallo Pinto.
   - Add slices or crumbles of Nicaraguan cheese on top of the beans and rice.
   - Optionally, serve with a dollop of crema (sour cream) on the side.
   - Garnish with chopped cilantro or green onions if desired.
5. **Serve:**
   - Serve the traditional Nicaraguan breakfast immediately while it's warm.
6. **Enjoy:**
   - Enjoy this hearty and flavorful breakfast, typically accompanied by a cup of coffee or fruit juice.

This breakfast dish is customizable, so feel free to adjust the quantities or add other traditional Nicaraguan elements like corn tortillas, avocado slices, or a side of fried cheese.

Nacatamales

Serves: 9pcs Prep time: 2 hrs Cook time: 3 hrs

INGREDIENTS

For the Filling:

1 1/2 pounds of pork shoulder or beef chuck, cut into small pieces

1 cup of cooked rice

1/2 cup of cooked red beans (or black beans)

2 cloves of garlic, minced

1 onion, finely chopped

1 red bell pepper, finely chopped

1 green bell pepper, finely chopped

2 tomatoes, diced

1/2 cup of raisins

1/2 cup of pitted green olives, sliced

1/4 cup of capers

1/4 cup of vegetable oil

1/2 teaspoon of ground cumin

1/2 teaspoon of ground achiote (annatto) for color (optional)
Salt and black pepper, to taste
Fresh cilantro and parsley, chopped, for garnish

For the Corn Dough:

4 cups of masa harina (corn dough)
1 cup of vegetable oil
2 1/2 cups of chicken or beef broth
1/2 teaspoon of baking powder
Salt, to taste

For Assembling:

Banana leaves (for wrapping)
Butcher's twine or kitchen string
Aluminum foil (optional)

DIRECTIONS

For the Filling:

1. **Sauté the Aromatics:**
   - In a large skillet, heat the vegetable oil over medium-high heat.
   - Add the finely chopped onion and cook until it becomes translucent.
   - Stir in the minced garlic, chopped red and green bell peppers, and diced tomatoes. Sauté until they are soft and fragrant.
2. **Cook the Meat:**
   - Add the meat pieces to the skillet and cook until they are browned.
   - Season the meat with ground cumin, ground achiote (if using), salt, and black pepper.
   - Stir in the cooked rice, cooked beans, raisins, olives, and capers.
   - Cook the mixture for about 15-20 minutes, allowing the flavors to meld. The filling should be moist but not too liquidy.

For the Corn Dough:

1. Prepare the Dough:
    - In a large mixing bowl, combine the masa harina, vegetable oil, chicken or beef broth, baking powder, and salt.
    - Knead the mixture until it forms a smooth and slightly firm dough. Adjust the consistency by adding more masa harina or broth as needed.

For Assembling:

1. Prepare the Banana Leaves:
    - Soak the banana leaves in warm water for a few minutes to soften them.
    - Cut the leaves into rectangular pieces, about 10-12 inches wide.
2. Assemble the Nacatamales:
    - Place a banana leaf rectangle on a flat surface.
    - Spread a small amount of corn dough onto the center of the leaf, forming a rectangular shape.
    - Add a portion of the filling on top of the corn dough.
    - Fold the banana leaf over the filling to create a rectangular packet.
    - Fold in the sides and tie the nacatamal with kitchen twine or kitchen string.
    - If desired, you can wrap the nacatamal in aluminum foil for added stability.
3. Steam the Nacatamales:
    - Arrange the nacatamales in a large steamer or a large pot with a steaming insert.
    - Steam the nacatamales over simmering water for about 2-3 hours, or until the dough is fully cooked.
4. Serve:
    - Carefully unwrap the nacatamales and serve them hot.
    - Garnish with chopped fresh cilantro and parsley.

Nicaraguan Nacatamales are a traditional and flavorful dish, often enjoyed for special occasions or as a hearty meal. The combination of tender meat, savory fillings, and corn dough wrapped in banana leaves is a culinary delight. Enjoy!

Indio Viejo

Serves: 6-8 Prep time: 20 min Cook time: 1 hr

INGREDIENTS

For the Soup:

2 pounds of chicken, beef, or pork (your choice), cut into pieces

2 cups of masa harina (corn dough)

1 onion, finely chopped

2 cloves of garlic, minced

1 red bell pepper, finely chopped

1 green bell pepper, finely chopped

2 tomatoes, diced

3 tablespoons of vegetable oil

2 tablespoons of achiote (annatto) paste or powder

1/2 cup of fresh sour orange juice (if unavailable, use a mixture of orange and lime juice)

4 cups of water or chicken broth

2-3 sprigs of fresh cilantro

2-3 sprigs of fresh parsley

Salt and black pepper, to taste

For Garnish:

Sliced red onions and thinly sliced jalapeño rings

Lime wedges

DIRECTIONS

1. **Sauté the Aromatics:**
   - In a large, heavy-bottomed pot, heat the vegetable oil over medium-high heat.
   - Add the finely chopped onion and cook until it becomes translucent.
   - Stir in the minced garlic, chopped red and green bell peppers, and diced tomatoes. Sauté until they are soft and fragrant.
2. **Cook the Meat:**
   - Add the chicken, beef, or pork pieces to the pot and cook until they are browned.
   - Season the meat with salt and black pepper.
3. **Prepare the Masa:**
   - In a separate bowl, mix the masa harina with water to form a smooth, thick paste.
4. **Add Achiote and Masa:**
   - Add the achiote paste or powder to the pot, stirring to combine.
   - Pour in the masa mixture and continue stirring to prevent lumps.
5. **Combine with Sour Orange Juice:**
   - Stir in the fresh sour orange juice (or the mixture of orange and lime juice).
   - Mix until all the ingredients are well combined.
6. **Add Liquid and Herbs:**
   - Pour in the water or chicken broth to the pot and add the sprigs of fresh cilantro and parsley.
   - Let the soup simmer for about 30-45 minutes, allowing the flavors to meld. The soup should thicken as it cooks.

7. **Serve:**

- Serve Nicaraguan Indio Viejo hot, garnished with sliced red onions and thinly sliced jalapeño rings.
- Offer lime wedges on the side.

Nicaraguan Indio Viejo is a flavorful and hearty stew that combines meat, corn masa, and aromatic spices. It's a beloved dish in Nicaragua, often enjoyed during special occasions and family gatherings. Enjoy!

Guirilas

Serves: 4-6 Prep time: 20 min Cook time: 20 min

INGREDIENTS

2 cups of fresh corn kernels (you can also use frozen corn)

1/2 cup of masa harina (corn flour)

2 tablespoons of all-purpose flour

1/4 cup of milk

1/4 cup of grated queso duro (hard cheese), such as queso seco

1/4 cup of crumbled queso fresco (fresh cheese)

1/4 cup of finely chopped green bell pepper

1/4 cup of finely chopped white onion

1/4 cup of chopped fresh cilantro

2 cloves of garlic, minced

1/2 teaspoon of baking powder

1/2 teaspoon of achiote (annatto) paste or powder for color (optional)

Salt and black pepper, to taste

Vegetable oil for frying

DIRECTIONS

1. **Prepare the Corn Mixture:**
    - In a blender, combine the fresh corn kernels with the milk. Blend until you have a smooth corn puree.
2. **Mix the Ingredients:**
    - In a large mixing bowl, combine the corn puree, masa harina, all-purpose flour, grated queso duro, crumbled queso fresco, green bell pepper, white onion, chopped cilantro, minced garlic, baking powder, achiote paste or powder (if using), and salt and black pepper to taste.
3. **Form the Guirilas:**
    - Heat a non-stick skillet or griddle over medium-high heat and lightly grease it with vegetable oil.
    - Take a portion of the corn mixture and form it into a ball. Flatten it into a round patty about 1/2 inch thick. Repeat with the remaining mixture.
4. **Cook the Guirilas:**
    - Place the guirilas on the hot skillet and cook for about 4-5 minutes on each side, or until they are golden brown and cooked through. You may need to add a little more oil to the skillet when you flip them.
5. **Serve:**
    - Serve Nicaraguan Guirilas hot as a delicious and crispy side dish or snack.

Nicaraguan Guirilas are a delightful combination of fresh corn, cheese, and seasonings, creating a savory and crispy treat that's perfect for any occasion. Enjoy!

Vigoron

Serves: 4-6 Prep time: 30 min Cook time: 20 min

INGREDIENTS

For the Yuca (Cassava) Salad:

2 pounds of yuca (cassava), peeled and cut into bite-sized chunks

1/2 cup of white vinegar

Salt, to taste

2 cups of chicharrones (crispy fried pork rinds)

1/2 cup of pickled cabbage (curtido)

1/2 cup of diced tomatoes

1/4 cup of thinly sliced green bell pepper

1/4 cup of thinly sliced white onion

For the Salsa:

2-3 small chili peppers (such as chiltepe or habanero), finely chopped (adjust to your preferred level of spiciness)

1/4 cup of fresh lime juice

Salt, to taste

DIRECTIONS

For the Yuca Salad:

1. **Boil the Yuca:**
   - In a large pot, bring water to a boil and add the yuca chunks.
   - Cook the yuca for about 15-20 minutes or until it's tender when pierced with a fork.
   - Drain the yuca and allow it to cool slightly.
2. **Marinate with Vinegar:**
   - While the yuca is still warm, place it in a large mixing bowl.
   - Pour the white vinegar over the yuca and sprinkle with salt.
   - Gently toss to combine, allowing the yuca to absorb the flavors.
3. **Assemble the Vigorón:**
   - On a serving platter, arrange a layer of marinated yuca.
   - Top with a generous amount of chicharrones (crispy fried pork rinds).
   - Add pickled cabbage (curtido), diced tomatoes, sliced green bell pepper, and sliced white onion on top.

For the Salsa:

1. **Prepare the Salsa:**
   - In a separate bowl, mix the finely chopped chili peppers with fresh lime juice.
   - Season with salt to taste.
2. **Serve:**
   - Serve Nicaraguan Vigorón with the chili pepper salsa on the side.
   - Enjoy this delightful and flavorful combination of yuca, chicharrones, and pickled vegetables.

Nicaraguan Vigorón is a traditional and delicious dish that offers a delightful mix of textures and flavors. It's perfect for a quick snack or a light meal. Enjoy!

Arroz Aguado

Serves: 6-8 Prep time: 15 min Cook time: 45 min

INGREDIENTS

1 whole chicken, cut into pieces (or 4-6 chicken thighs)

2 cups rice, rinsed

1 onion, finely chopped

3 cloves garlic, minced

1 bell pepper, diced

2 tomatoes, diced

1 carrot, diced

1 chayote or zucchini, diced

1 teaspoon ground cumin

1 teaspoon dried oregano

8 cups chicken broth or water

2 tablespoons vegetable oil

Salt and pepper to taste

Fresh cilantro for garnish

Lime wedges for serving (optional)

DIRECTIONS

1. **Prepare the Chicken:**
    - Rinse the chicken pieces under cold water and pat them dry with paper towels. Season the chicken with salt and pepper.
2. **Brown the Chicken:**
    - Heat vegetable oil in a large pot or Dutch oven over medium-high heat. Brown the chicken pieces on all sides until they develop a golden-brown color. Remove the chicken from the pot and set it aside.
3. **Sauté Aromatics and Vegetables:**
    - In the same pot, add the chopped onion, minced garlic, and diced bell pepper. Sauté until they soften.
    - Add the diced tomatoes, carrot, and chayote or zucchini into the pot. Cook for a few more minutes until the vegetables begin to soften.
4. **Add Seasonings and Chicken:**
    - Return the browned chicken pieces back into the pot with the sautéed vegetables.
    - Sprinkle ground cumin, dried oregano, salt, and pepper over the chicken and vegetables.
5. **Cook the Rice:**
    - Pour in the chicken broth or water into the pot, covering the chicken and vegetables.
    - Add the rinsed rice to the pot. Stir gently to combine all the ingredients.
    - Bring the mixture to a boil, then reduce the heat to low. Cover the pot and let it simmer for about 30-35 minutes until the rice is cooked and the chicken is tender.
6. **Serve:**
    - Once the Arroz Aguado is ready, taste and adjust the seasoning if necessary.
    - Serve the soup hot in bowls, ensuring each serving has a mix of chicken, vegetables, and rice.
    - Garnish with fresh cilantro and serve with lime wedges for squeezing over the soup before eating, if desired.

Arroz Aguado is a wholesome and comforting dish, perfect for a hearty meal. Adjust the seasoning and vegetables according to your preferences. Enjoy your homemade Nicaraguan Arroz Aguado!

Tostones

Serves: 4-6 Prep time: 15 min Cook time: 15 min

INGREDIENTS

2 green plantains

Vegetable or canola oil for frying

Salt to taste

Garlic powder or minced garlic (optional)

Water

Paper towels

DIRECTIONS

1. **Prepare the Plantains:**
   - Peel the plantains by slicing off both ends and making a lengthwise slit along the ridges of the plantain skin. Carefully peel the skin off the plantains.
2. **Cut and Soak:**
   - Cut the peeled plantains into 1-inch thick slices.
   - In a bowl, mix water with a little salt. Soak the plantain slices in this saltwater solution for about 10 minutes. This helps remove excess starch.

3. **Fry the Plantain Slices:**

- Heat vegetable or canola oil in a frying pan over medium-high heat.
- Pat the soaked plantain slices dry with paper towels.
- Carefully place the plantain slices into the hot oil and fry them for about 2-3 minutes on each side until they are lightly golden but not fully cooked through.
- Remove the partially cooked plantain slices from the oil and place them on a paper towel-lined plate to drain excess oil. Let them cool slightly.

4. **Flatten and Fry Again:**

- Using a tostonera (if available) or a flat-bottomed object like a jar or glass, flatten each partially cooked plantain slice into a disc, about ¼ to ½ inch thick.
- Return the flattened plantain slices back into the hot oil and fry them again for about 2-3 minutes on each side until they turn golden brown and crispy.
- Remove the tostones from the oil and place them on paper towels to drain excess oil.

5. **Season and Serve:**

- While still hot, sprinkle the tostones with salt and garlic powder or minced garlic (optional) for added flavor.
- Serve the Nicaraguan Tostones immediately as a side dish or snack.

Tostones are typically served as a side dish or appetizer and are enjoyed with a variety of dips or alongside main courses. Adjust the seasoning according to your taste preferences. Enjoy your homemade Nicaraguan Tostones!

Rosquillas de Queso

Serves: 24pcs   Prep time: 20 min   Cook time: 15 min

INGREDIENTS

2 cups all-purpose flour

1 cup grated cheese (queso seco or Parmesan cheese works well)

1 teaspoon baking powder

1/2 cup unsalted butter, at room temperature

1/2 cup granulated sugar

2 eggs

1 teaspoon vanilla extract

Zest of 1 lemon or orange (optional)

Additional sugar for rolling (optional)

DIRECTIONS

1. Preheat the Oven:

- Preheat your oven to 350°F (175°C). Line baking sheets with parchment paper or lightly grease them.

2. **Mix Dry Ingredients:**
   - In a mixing bowl, whisk together the all-purpose flour, baking powder, and grated cheese until well combined. Set aside.
3. **Cream Butter and Sugar:**
   - In a separate bowl, cream together the room temperature butter and granulated sugar until smooth and creamy.
4. **Combine Wet and Dry Ingredients:**
   - Add the eggs, vanilla extract, and lemon or orange zest (if using) to the creamed butter and sugar. Mix until well combined.
   - Gradually add the dry ingredients (flour, baking powder, and cheese) to the wet mixture. Stir until a dough forms. It might be slightly crumbly, but it should hold together when pressed.
5. **Shape the Cookies:**
   - Take small portions of the dough and roll them into small balls, about 1 inch in diameter.
   - Place each ball of dough onto the prepared baking sheets, leaving some space between them as they will slightly spread while baking.
6. **Flatten and Decorate (optional):**
   - Using a fork, gently press down on each cookie ball to flatten it slightly. You can also make a crisscross pattern with the fork for decoration.
   - Optionally, you can sprinkle some granulated sugar on top of the cookies before baking for added sweetness and texture.
7. **Bake the Cookies:**
   - Place the baking sheets in the preheated oven and bake the Rosquillos de Queso for about 12-15 minutes or until they turn golden brown around the edges.
   - Once baked, remove the cookies from the oven and let them cool on the baking sheets for a few minutes before transferring them to a wire rack to cool completely.
8. **Serve:**
   - Once cooled, serve and enjoy these delightful Nicaraguan cheese cookies!

Rosquillos de Queso are wonderful as a snack or dessert, pairing perfectly with coffee or tea. You can store them in an airtight container for a few days to keep them fresh. Adjust the sweetness by adding more or less sugar to suit your taste.

Section 7

Panama

Sancocho de Gallina

Serves: 6-8 Prep time: 30 min Cook time: 2 hrs

INGREDIENTS

For the Soup:

1 whole chicken, cut into pieces

8 cups of water

1 onion, chopped

2 cloves of garlic, minced

1 green bell pepper, chopped

1 red bell pepper, chopped

1 cup of fresh corn kernels (or frozen corn)

1 cup of peeled yuca (cassava), cut into chunks

1 cup of peeled ñame (yam), cut into chunks

1 cup of peeled otoe (squat palm fruit), cut into chunks (optional)

2 ripe plantains, peeled and sliced into thick rounds

2 tablespoons of vegetable oil

2 ears of corn, each cut into 3-4 pieces

Salt and black pepper, to taste

For the Salsa:

1 small onion, finely chopped

2 tablespoons of fresh cilantro, chopped

1 teaspoon of fresh lime juice

Salt and pepper, to taste

DIRECTIONS

For the Soup:

1. **Prepare the Chicken:**
   - In a large soup pot, combine the chicken pieces, water, chopped onion, minced garlic, and a pinch of salt.
   - Bring the mixture to a boil, then reduce the heat and simmer for about 30 minutes, or until the chicken is tender.
2. **Add Vegetables:**
   - Add the green and red bell peppers, fresh (or frozen) corn kernels, yuca, ñame, and otoe (if using) to the pot.
   - Continue to simmer for an additional 20-25 minutes, or until the vegetables are tender.
3. **Fry the Plantains:**
   - In a separate skillet, heat the vegetable oil over medium-high heat.
   - Fry the plantain slices until they are golden and crispy on both sides. Remove and drain on paper towels.
4. **Add Corn Ears:**
   - Place the corn ear pieces into the pot and simmer for another 10-15 minutes.
5. **Season:**
   - Season the Sancocho with salt and black pepper to taste. Adjust the seasoning as needed.

For the Salsa:

- Prepare the Salsa:
    - In a small bowl, combine the finely chopped onion, fresh cilantro, fresh lime juice, salt, and pepper. Mix well.
- Serve:
    - Serve Panamanian Sancocho de Gallina hot, garnished with the plantain slices and a dollop of the prepared salsa on top.

Panamanian Sancocho de Gallina is a hearty and flavorful chicken soup with a mix of vegetables and a touch of acidity from the salsa. It's a traditional dish enjoyed in Panama and is often served during special occasions and gatherings. Enjoy!

Ropa Vieja

Serves: 6 Prep time: 20 min Cook time: 2.5 hrs

INGREDIENTS

For the Beef:

2 pounds of flank steak or skirt steak

1 onion, chopped

1 green bell pepper, chopped

1 red bell pepper, chopped

3 cloves of garlic, minced

1 can (14 ounces) of diced tomatoes

1/4 cup of tomato sauce

2 cups of beef broth

1 bay leaf

1 teaspoon of ground cumin

1 teaspoon of dried oregano

Salt and black pepper, to taste

Vegetable oil for searing

For the Sofrito:

1 onion, chopped

1 green bell pepper, chopped

3 cloves of garlic, minced

1/4 cup of tomato sauce

1/4 cup of cooking oil

DIRECTIONS

1. **Sear the Beef:**
   - In a large Dutch oven or heavy-bottomed pot, heat some vegetable oil over medium-high heat.
   - Sear the flank steak on both sides until it's browned. Remove the steak from the pot and set it aside.
2. **Prepare the Beef Sauce:**
   - In the same pot, add chopped onion and garlic. Sauté until they're soft and fragrant.
   - Stir in the diced tomatoes, tomato sauce, beef broth, bay leaf, ground cumin, dried oregano, salt, and black pepper.
   - Return the seared beef to the pot and cover it with the sauce.
   - Bring the mixture to a boil, then reduce the heat to low. Cover and simmer for about 1.5-2 hours, or until the beef is tender and can be easily shredded.
3. **Shred the Beef:**
   - Remove the cooked beef from the pot and shred it with two forks.
4. **Prepare the Sofrito:**
   - In a separate skillet, heat cooking oil over medium-high heat.
   - Sauté the chopped onion, green bell pepper, and minced garlic until they are soft and tender.
   - Add 1/4 cup of tomato sauce to the skillet and mix it in with the sofrito.
5. **Combine the Sofrito and Shredded Beef:**
   - Add the shredded beef to the sofrito mixture and stir to combine. Cook for an additional 10-15 minutes to let the flavors meld.

6. **Serve:**

- Panamanian Ropa Vieja is typically served hot over white rice, accompanied by side dishes like fried plantains and black beans.

Panamanian Ropa Vieja is a delicious and comforting dish made from tender shredded beef in a rich tomato sauce. It's a popular and hearty meal in Panama. Enjoy!

Carimanolas

Serves: 6pcs Prep time: 30 min Cook time: 45 min

INGREDIENTS

For the Dough:

2 cups of mashed yuca (cassava)

1/4 cup of vegetable oil

1/4 cup of warm chicken or vegetable broth

Salt, to taste

For the Filling:

1 cup of ground beef or pork

1 small onion, finely chopped

1 small red bell pepper, finely chopped

2 cloves of garlic, minced

1/2 teaspoon of ground cumin

1/2 teaspoon of dried oregano

Salt and black pepper, to taste

Vegetable oil for sautéing

For Assembling:

2 hard-boiled eggs, sliced into rounds (optional)

1 cup of vegetable oil for frying

DIRECTIONS

For the Filling:

1. **Prepare the Filling:**
    - In a skillet, heat some vegetable oil over medium-high heat.
    - Sauté the finely chopped onion and red bell pepper until they are soft and translucent.
    - Add the minced garlic, ground beef (or pork), ground cumin, dried oregano, salt, and black pepper.
    - Cook the filling until the meat is browned and fully cooked, breaking it into smaller pieces with a spatula as it cooks.
    - Remove the skillet from the heat and set the filling aside.

For the Dough:

1. **Prepare the Yuca Dough:**
    - In a large mixing bowl, combine the mashed yuca, vegetable oil, warm chicken or vegetable broth, and salt.
    - Mix until you have a smooth, pliable dough.

Assembling the Carimanolas:

1. **Shape the Dough:**
    - Divide the yuca dough into 6 equal portions.
    - Take one portion of dough and flatten it in your hand to form a round disc.
2. **Add the Filling:**
    - Place a spoonful of the prepared filling in the center of the dough disc.
    - Optionally, add a slice of hard-boiled egg.
3. **Fold and Seal:**
    - Carefully fold the dough over the filling to form a half-moon shape.
    - Gently press the edges to seal the carimanola.

4. **Fry the Carimanolas:**
    - In a deep skillet or frying pan, heat vegetable oil over medium-high heat.
    - Fry the carimanolas until they are golden brown and crispy, about 3-4 minutes on each side.
    - Remove them from the oil and place them on paper towels to drain any excess oil.
5. **Serve:**
- Panamanian Carimanolas are typically served hot and can be enjoyed as a snack or a light meal.

Panamanian Carimanolas are a flavorful and hearty dish with a crispy exterior and a delicious filling. They are a beloved snack in Panama, often enjoyed with hot sauce or other condiments. Enjoy!

Ron Ponche

Serves: 8-10 Prep time: 15 min Cook time: 10 min

INGREDIENTS

1 can (12 oz) evaporated milk

1 can (14 oz) condensed milk

1 cup dark rum (adjust to taste)

4 egg yolks

1 teaspoon vanilla extract

1 teaspoon ground nutmeg

1 teaspoon ground cinnamon

1 cup water

1 cup sugar (adjust to taste)

Additional nutmeg and cinnamon for garnish (optional)

DIRECTIONS

1. **Prepare the Base:**
   - In a saucepan, combine the water and sugar. Heat over medium heat, stirring constantly, until the sugar completely dissolves. Let this simple syrup cool.
2. **Beat the Egg Yolks:**
   - In a separate mixing bowl, beat the egg yolks until they become pale and slightly thickened.
3. **Mix the Ingredients:**
   - In a blender or large mixing bowl, combine the evaporated milk, condensed milk, dark rum, vanilla extract, ground nutmeg, and ground cinnamon.
   - Slowly add the cooled simple syrup to this mixture and blend or mix well until everything is thoroughly combined.
4. **Temper the Eggs:**
   - Gradually add a small amount of the milk mixture into the beaten egg yolks while continuously whisking. This process, called tempering, prevents the eggs from curdling when added to the warm mixture.
5. **Combine and Heat:**
   - Pour the tempered egg mixture back into the rest of the milk mixture and stir thoroughly.
   - Transfer the combined mixture to a saucepan and cook over low heat, stirring constantly, until the mixture thickens slightly. Be cautious not to boil it; the goal is to heat it gently.
6. **Chill and Serve:**
   - Remove the mixture from the heat and let it cool to room temperature.
   - Once cooled, transfer the Ron Ponche to a pitcher or container and refrigerate it for a few hours or overnight until it's well chilled.
   - Before serving, stir the Ron Ponche well and pour it into glasses.
   - Optionally, sprinkle a little ground nutmeg and cinnamon on top for garnish.
7. **Enjoy:**
   - Serve the chilled Panamanian Ron Ponche as a festive holiday drink for celebrations and gatherings.

This creamy and spiced beverage is perfect for festive occasions in Panama. The recipe can be adjusted to suit your taste preferences regarding sweetness and spice levels. Enjoy responsibly!

Patacones

Serves: 4 Prep time: 20 min Cook time: 15 min

INGREDIENTS

4 green (unripe) plantains

Vegetable oil for frying

Salt, to taste

DIRECTIONS

1. **Prepare the Plantains:**
   - Start by peeling the green plantains. Cut off the ends and make a lengthwise slit through the skin, being careful not to cut into the flesh. Then, remove the skin.
2. **Cut the Plantains:**
   - Cut the peeled plantains into rounds, each about 1-1.5 inches thick.
3. **Heat the Oil:**
   - In a deep skillet or frying pan, heat enough vegetable oil to submerge the plantain rounds.

4. **Fry the Plantains:**
   - When the oil is hot (around 350°F or 175°C), carefully add the plantain rounds to the oil in batches. Be cautious to avoid overcrowding the pan.
   - Fry the plantains for about 2-3 minutes on each side, or until they become lightly golden and slightly softened.
   - Using a slotted spoon or tongs, remove the partially fried plantains from the oil and place them on a paper towel-lined plate to drain excess oil.
5. **Flatten the Plantains:**
   - Take each partially fried plantain round and place it between two sheets of parchment paper or plastic wrap.
   - Using the bottom of a heavy glass or a flat utensil, press down on the plantain to flatten it to about half its original thickness.
6. **Re-fry the Plantains:**
   - Return the flattened plantains to the hot oil and fry them again for about 2-3 minutes on each side, or until they are golden brown, crispy, and fully cooked.
   - Once done, remove the patacones from the oil and place them on fresh paper towels to drain any excess oil.
7. **Season and Serve:**
   - While the patacones are still hot, sprinkle them with salt to taste.

Panamanian Patacones are a popular and delicious snack or side dish made from green plantains. They are crispy on the outside and tender on the inside, perfect for dipping in various sauces or serving alongside your favorite Panamanian dishes. Enjoy!

Corn Tortillas

Serves: 13pcs Prep time: 15 min Cook time: 25 min

INGREDIENTS

2 cups masa harina (corn flour)

1 ½ cups warm water

Pinch of salt (optional)

DIRECTIONS

1. **Prepare the Dough:**
    - In a mixing bowl, combine the masa harina (corn flour) and a pinch of salt, if using.
    - Slowly pour the warm water into the masa harina while mixing it with a fork or your hands. Knead the mixture until it forms a smooth, pliable dough. If the dough is too dry, add a little more water, one tablespoon at a time. If it's too wet, add a bit more masa harina.
2. **Rest the Dough:**
    - Once the dough is formed, cover it with a clean kitchen towel or plastic wrap and let it rest for about 10-15 minutes. This allows the masa to hydrate fully and makes it easier to work with.

3. **Shape the Tortillas:**
   - Divide the dough into golf ball-sized portions and roll each portion into a smooth ball.
   - If you have a tortilla press, line it with plastic wrap or parchment paper. Place a ball of dough in the center, cover it with another piece of plastic, and press down to flatten it into a round tortilla. If you don't have a press, use a rolling pin to flatten the dough between two sheets of plastic or parchment paper.
4. **Cook the Tortillas:**
   - Heat a non-stick skillet or griddle over medium-high heat.
   - Carefully place the flattened tortilla onto the hot skillet or griddle. Cook for about 1-2 minutes on each side until it starts to puff slightly and develops light brown spots.
   - Flip the tortilla and cook the other side. Press down gently with a spatula if needed to help it cook evenly.
   - Remove the cooked tortilla from the skillet and stack them on a clean kitchen towel or in a tortilla warmer to keep them warm and soft while you cook the remaining tortillas.
5. Serve:
   - Serve the warm Panamanian Corn Tortillas with your favorite dishes or fill them with various ingredients for tacos, quesadillas, or wraps.

Freshly made corn tortillas are a versatile and delicious addition to many meals. They're best enjoyed when warm and can be used immediately or stored in a sealed container or plastic bag for a day or two.

Hojaldra

Serves: 6pcs Prep time: 15 min Cook time: 15 min

INGREDIENTS

3 cups of all-purpose flour

1 teaspoon of baking powder

1/2 teaspoon of salt

1/4 cup of vegetable oil

1/2 cup of water (approximately)

Vegetable oil for frying

DIRECTIONS

1. Prepare the Dough:
   - In a mixing bowl, combine the all-purpose flour, baking powder, and salt.
   - Add the vegetable oil and mix it into the dry ingredients until the mixture resembles coarse crumbs.

2. **Form the Dough:**
   - Gradually add water while kneading the dough until it comes together and is smooth and elastic. The amount of water needed may vary, so add it slowly.
   - Form the dough into a ball, cover it with a clean cloth, and let it rest for about 10 minutes.
3. **Roll Out the Dough:**
   - On a lightly floured surface, roll out the dough into a thin sheet, about 1/8 inch thick.
4. **Cut the Hojaldras:**
   - Use a round cutter or a glass to cut the rolled-out dough into circles or rounds.
5. **Create the Signature Design:**
   - Use a smaller round cutter or the back of a decorating tip to create a smaller circle in the center of each hojaldra.
6. **Fry the Hojaldras:**
   - In a deep skillet or frying pan, heat vegetable oil over medium-high heat. The oil should be about 350°F (175°C).
   - Carefully add the hojaldras to the hot oil, a few at a time.
   - Fry them for about 2-3 minutes on each side or until they are golden brown and crispy.
   - Remove the hojaldras from the oil and place them on paper towels to drain any excess oil.
7. **Serve:**
   - Panamanian Hojaldras are best served warm and can be enjoyed on their own or with a drizzle of honey, powdered sugar, or a sprinkle of salt.

Panamanian Hojaldra is a delightful, deep-fried pastry known for its crispy texture and delicious taste. It is a popular snack and breakfast treat in Panama. Enjoy!

Guacho

Serves: 4-6 Prep time: 20 min Cook time: 45 min

INGREDIENTS

For the Guacho:

1 cup of rice

1 cup of green pigeon peas (guandu or gandules)

1 pound of boneless chicken, pork, or a combination, cut into small pieces

1/2 cup of onion, finely chopped

1/2 cup of bell pepper (red or green), finely chopped

2 cloves of garlic, minced

2 tablespoons of vegetable oil

1 teaspoon of achiote (annatto) paste or powder for color (optional)

1 teaspoon of ground cumin

1/2 teaspoon of dried oregano

4 cups of water

Salt and black pepper, to taste

For Serving:

Slices of lime or lemon

Sliced radishes (optional)

DIRECTIONS

1. **Prepare the Pigeon Peas:**
   - In a bowl, soak the green pigeon peas in water for about 30 minutes. Drain and set aside.
2. **Sauté the Meat:**
   - In a large pot, heat the vegetable oil over medium-high heat.
   - Add the finely chopped onion, bell pepper, and minced garlic. Sauté until they are soft and fragrant.
3. **Brown the Meat:**
   - Add the chicken, pork, or a combination of both to the pot.
   - Brown the meat on all sides, stirring occasionally.
4. **Add Seasonings:**
   - Stir in the achiote paste or powder (if using), ground cumin, dried oregano, salt, and black pepper.
5. **Add Rice and Peas:**
   - Add the rice and drained pigeon peas to the pot. Stir to combine with the meat and seasonings.
6. **Add Water:**
   - Pour in the water and bring the mixture to a boil.
7. **Simmer:**
   - Reduce the heat to low, cover the pot, and let the Guacho simmer for about 30-40 minutes, or until the rice is cooked and the liquid is absorbed. You may need to stir occasionally to prevent sticking.

8. Serve:

- Serve Panamanian Guacho hot, garnished with slices of lime or lemon.
- Optionally, you can add sliced radishes for a refreshing crunch.

Panamanian Guacho is a comforting and hearty one-pot dish that combines rice, pigeon-peas, and your choice of meat, seasoned with aromatic spices. It's a popular and satisfying meal in Panama. Enjoy!

Pargo Frito

Serves: 4 Prep time: 15 min Cook time: 20 min

INGREDIENTS

2 whole red snappers, cleaned and scaled (about 1.5-2 lbs each)

1 cup all-purpose flour

1 teaspoon garlic powder

1 teaspoon onion powder

1 teaspoon paprika

Salt and pepper to taste

Vegetable oil for frying

Lime wedges for serving

Optional: chopped cilantro or parsley for garnish

DIRECTIONS

1. **Prep the Red Snappers:**
   - Rinse the red snappers thoroughly under cold water and pat them dry using paper towels.
   - Make 2-3 diagonal cuts on each side of the fish with a sharp knife. This helps the fish cook evenly and allows the seasonings to penetrate.
2. **Season and Coat the Fish:**
   - In a shallow dish, mix together the flour, garlic powder, onion powder, paprika, salt, and pepper.
   - Dredge each red snapper in the seasoned flour mixture, ensuring it's coated evenly on both sides. Shake off any excess flour.
3. **Heat the Oil:**
   - In a large skillet or frying pan, pour enough vegetable oil to cover the bottom by about half an inch. Heat the oil over medium-high heat until it's hot but not smoking (around 350-375°F or 175-190°C).
4. **Fry the Red Snappers:**
   - Carefully place the seasoned red snappers in the hot oil. Depending on the size of your skillet, you may need to fry them one at a time or in batches to avoid overcrowding.
   - Fry each side of the fish for about 5-7 minutes or until golden brown and crispy. Use kitchen tongs to gently flip the fish halfway through the cooking process.
   - Once cooked, transfer the fried red snappers to a plate lined with paper towels to drain excess oil.
5. **Serve:**
   - Serve the Pargo Frito hot with lime wedges on the side for squeezing over the fish.
   - Optionally, garnish with chopped cilantro or parsley for added freshness and flavor.
6. **Enjoy:**
   - Enjoy the Panamanian Pargo Frito as a delicious and crispy seafood dish, typically served with sides like rice, plantains, salad, or beans.

This dish is best served immediately after frying while the fish is still hot and crispy. Adjust the seasonings according to your taste preferences.

Conclusion

As our culinary journey through Central America comes to a flavorful close, we hope this cookbook has ignited a deep appreciation for the rich tapestry of tastes, aromas, and traditions that define this vibrant region. From the comforting warmth of a bowl of sopa de frijoles to the zest of a fresh ceviche, each dish carries within it the stories of generations and the essence of a land deeply connected to its roots.

Our exploration of Central American cuisine has been more than just a collection of recipes; it's been a celebration of cultural heritage and the art of bringing people together. As you've navigated these pages and recreated these traditional dishes in your own kitchen, we hope you've experienced the joy of discovery—the joy of exploring new flavors, embracing authenticity, and sharing meals that speak the language of tradition.

May the flavors linger in your memories, reminding you of the diverse and vibrant culinary landscapes of Central America. Keep these recipes close to your heart, sharing them with friends and family, and keeping alive the spirit of this captivating region's cuisine.

Thank you for joining us on this gastronomic journey—a journey woven with the spices, stories, and warmth of Central America's kitchens.

¡Buen provecho y hasta luego! (Enjoy your meal and until next time!)

Your feedback is greatly appreciated!

It's through your feedback, support and reviews that I'm able to create the best books possible and serve more people.

I would be extremely grateful if you could take just 60 seconds to kindly leave an honest review of the book on Amazon. Please share your feedback and thoughts for others to see.

To do so, simply find the book on Amazon's website (or wherever you purchased the book from) and locate the section to leave a review. Select a star rating and write a couple of sentences.

That's it! Thank you so much for your support.

Review this product

Share your thoughts with other customers

Write a customer review

References

- OpenAI. (2023). Conversations with ChatGPT. Retrieved 2023, from https://www.openai.com/chatgpt/

Made in the USA
Middletown, DE
26 November 2024

65501647R00106